CAMBRIDGE PRIMARY
Mathematics

Challenge

5

Name: ______________________________

Contents

Emma Low

CAMBRIDGE
UNIVERSITY PRESS

CAMBRIDGE
UNIVERSITY PRESS

University Printing House, Cambridge CB2 8BS, United Kingdom

One Liberty Plaza, 20th Floor, New York, NY 10006, USA

477 Williamstown Road, Port Melbourne, VIC 3207, Australia

314–321, 3rd Floor, Plot 3, Splendor Forum, Jasola District Centre, New Delhi - 110025, India

79 Anson Road, #06–04/06, Singapore 079906

Cambridge University Press is part of the University of Cambridge.

It furthers the University's mission by disseminating knowledge in the pursuit of education, learning and research at the highest international levels of excellence.

www.cambridge.org
Information on this title: education.cambridge.org/9781316509241

First published 2016

20 19 18 17 16 15 14 13 12 11 10 9 8 7 6

Printed in Great Britain by CPI Group (UK) Ltd, Croydon CR0 4YY

A catalogue record for this publication is available from the British Library

ISBN 978-1-316-50924-1 Paperback

Cambridge Primary Maths

This book is part of the Cambridge Primary Maths project. This is an innovative combination of curriculum and resources designed to support teachers and learners to succeed in primary mathematics through best-practice international maths teaching and a problem-solving approach.

To get involved, visit **www.cie.org.uk/cambridgeprimarymaths.**

Introduction

This *Challenge activity book* is part of a series of 12 write-in activity books for primary mathematics grades 1–6. It can be used as a standalone book, but the content also complements *Cambridge Primary Maths*. Learners progress at different rates, so this series provides a Challenge and Skills Builder activity book for each Primary Mathematics Curriculum Framework Stage to broaden the depth of and to support further learning.

The *Challenge* books extend learning by providing stretching activities to increase the depth of maths knowledge and skills. Support is given through short reminders of key information, topic vocabulary, and hints to prompt learning. These books have been written to support learners whose first language is not English.

How to use the books

The activities are for use by learners in school or at home, with adult support. Topics have been carefully chosen to focus on those areas where learners can stretch their depth of knowledge. The approach is linked directly to *Cambridge Primary Maths*, but teachers and parents can pick and choose which activities to cover, or go through the books in sequence.

The varied set of activities grow in challenge through each unit, including:

- closed questions with answers, so progress can be checked
- questions with more than one possible answer
- activities requiring resources, for example, dice, spinners or digit cards
- activities and games best done with someone else, in class or at home, which give the opportunity for parents and teachers to be fully involved in the child's learning
- activities to support different learning styles: working individually, in pairs, in groups
- A final section of Problems and puzzles is provided to challenge learners at the end of Grade 5.

How to approach the activities

Space is provided for learners to write their answers in the book. Some activities might need further practice or writing, so students could be given a blank notebook at the start of the year to use alongside the book. Each activity follows a standard structure.

- **Remember** gives an overview of key learning points. It introduces core concepts and, later, can be used as a revision guide. These sections should be read with an adult who can check that the learner understands the material before attempting the activities.
- **Vocabulary** assists with difficult mathematical terms, particularly when English is not the learner's first language. Learners should read through the key vocabulary. Where necessary, they should be encouraged to clarify their understanding by using a mathematical dictionary or by, ideally, seeking adult help.
- **Hints** prompt and assist in building understanding, and steer the learner in the right direction.
- **You will need** gives learners, teachers and parents a list of resources for each activity.
- **Photocopiable resources** are provided at the end of the book, for easy assembly in class or at home.
- **Links** to the Cambridge International Examinations Primary Mathematics Curriculum Framework objectives and the corresponding *Cambridge Primary Mathematics Teacher's Resource* are given in the footnote on every page.
- **Calculators** should be used to help learners understand numbers and the number system, including place value and properties of numbers. From Stage 5, learners are expected to become proficient in using calculators in appropriate situations. This book develops the learner's knowledge of number without a calculator, although calculators can be useful for checking work.

Note:

When a 'spinner' is included, put a paperclip flat on the page so the end is over the centre of the spinner. Place the pencil point in the centre of the spinner, through the paperclip. Hold the pencil firmly and spin the paperclip to generate a result.

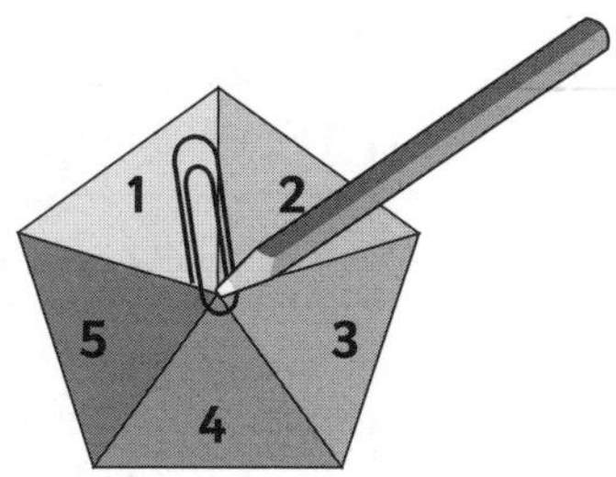

Tracking progress

Answers to closed questions are given at the back of the book – these allow teachers, parents and learners to check their work.

When completing each activity, teachers and parents are advised to encourage self-assessment by asking the students how straightforward they found the activity. When learners are reflecting on games, they should consider how challenging the mathematics was, not who won. Learners could use a ✓/ ✗ or red/green colouring system to record their self-assessment for each activity.

These assessments provide teachers and parents with an understanding of how best to support individual learners' next steps.

Place value and ordering

Remember

To solve these problems you need to understand that the position of a digit in a number is important to its value. Some of the positions are hundred thousands, ten thousands, thousands, hundreds, tens, ones, tenths.

< means 'is less than', > means 'is greater than'.

You will need: resource 1, page 76, counters for activity 1

Vocabulary

ten thousand, hundred thousand, multiple

1 **Starting numbers – a game for two players.**

Each player needs a place-value chart (resource 1) and 6 counters.

Players place their six counters on numbers on their place-value chart, one counter in each row. They should not allow their opponent to see their place-value chart.

Players find the total of the numbers they have covered on their place-value chart and record it here.

My total number ______________

Example: Counters placed on 200000, 40000, 2000, 700, 60 and 8 make a total of

242768.

100 000	200 000	300 000	400 000	500 000	600 000	700 000	800 000	900 000
10 000	20 000	30 000	40 000	50 000	60 000	70 000	80 000	90 000
1000	2000	3000	4000	5000	6000	7000	8000	9000
100	200	300	400	500	600	700	800	900
10	20	30	40	50	60	70	80	90
1	2	3	4	5	6	7	8	9

Take turns to say a number on the place-value chart. If your opponent has a counter on that number they give up their counter. Record the numbers in the table.

Players can have one guess at their opponent's total number after each turn. Record the guesses using the tables on the following page to help you.

The first player to correctly say their opponent's total number is the winner.

Hint: Record the guesses that you make so that you can eliminate numbers.

	Numbers guessed correctly
100 000s	
10 000s	
1000s	
100s	
10s	
1s	

My totals guessed				

2 A number has six digits.
It is an even number.
It is a multiple of 5.
The number rounds to 854 900 to the nearest 100.
The number is greater than eight hundred and fifty-four thousand, nine hundred and thirty.

What is the number? ________________

3 Order these numbers.

Write them in the spaces below.

658 107   74 922   609 999   841 624   742 229   88 043

☐☐☐■☐ < ☐☐☐☐■ < ☐☐■☐☐☐ < ☐■☐☐☐☐ < ■☐☐☐☐☐ < ☐☐☐■☐☐

Circle the value on the place-value chart below of the digits that appear in the shaded boxes.

100 000	200 000	300 000	400 000	500 000	600 000	700 000	800 000	900 000
10 000	20 000	30 000	40 000	50 000	60 000	70 000	80 000	90 000
1000	2000	3000	4000	5000	6000	7000	8000	9000
100	200	300	400	500	600	700	800	900
10	20	30	40	50	60	70	80	90
1	2	3	4	5	6	7	8	9

Find the total of the circled numbers on the place-value chart.

Show your working below.

4 Play this game with a partner, or an adult at home.

Take turns to choose a spinner to spin.

Choose to multiply or divide the number shown on the spinner by 10 or 100.

If the solution is on the grid of numbers, and not already covered, cover it with a counter.

If your opponent can show that you have placed a counter incorrectly, it is removed from the board.

The first player to have four counters in a row is the winner.

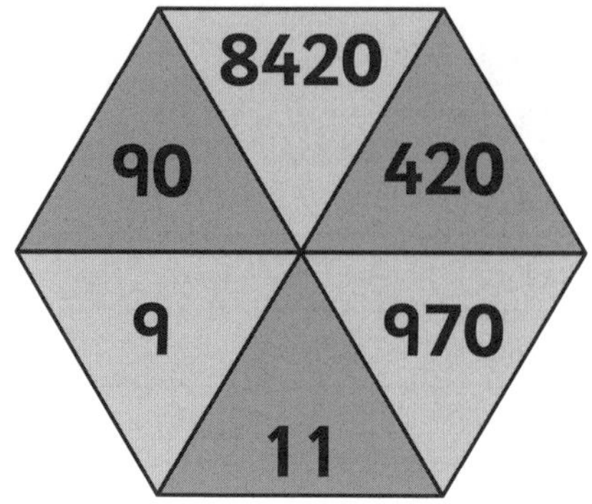

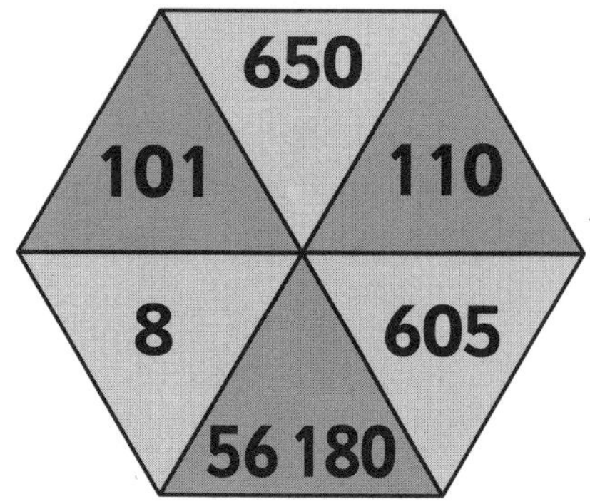

900	6.5	800	10 100
11 000	84.2	42	6050
561.8	9.7	65	1.1
842 000	60.5	97 000	4.2

Hint: Use the place-value chart below to help you multiply and divide.

hundred thousands	thousands	hundreds	tens	ones	• tenths
					•
					•
					•
					•
					•
					•
					•
					•

Rounding

Remember
Numbers can be rounded to 10, 100 and 1000. Imagine the number on a number line to help you decide which is the nearest. If the number is halfway between two rounding numbers always round up to the greater value.

Vocabulary
ten thousand, hundred thousand

1 Write some appropriate numbers in each section of the Venn diagrams.

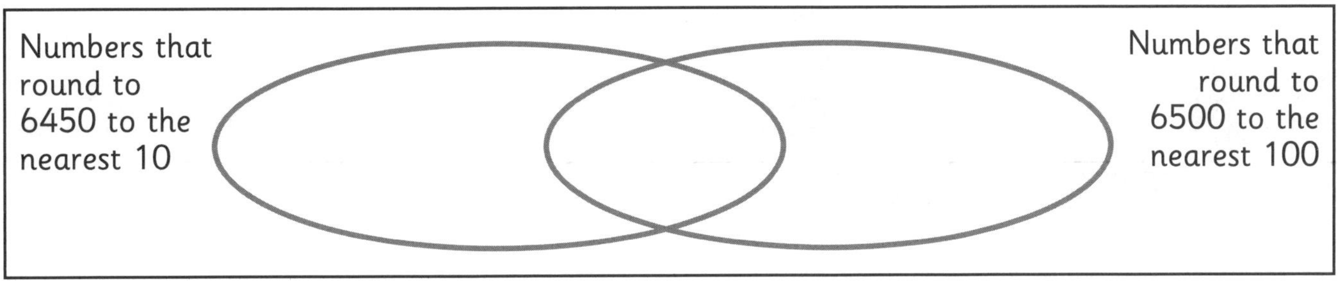

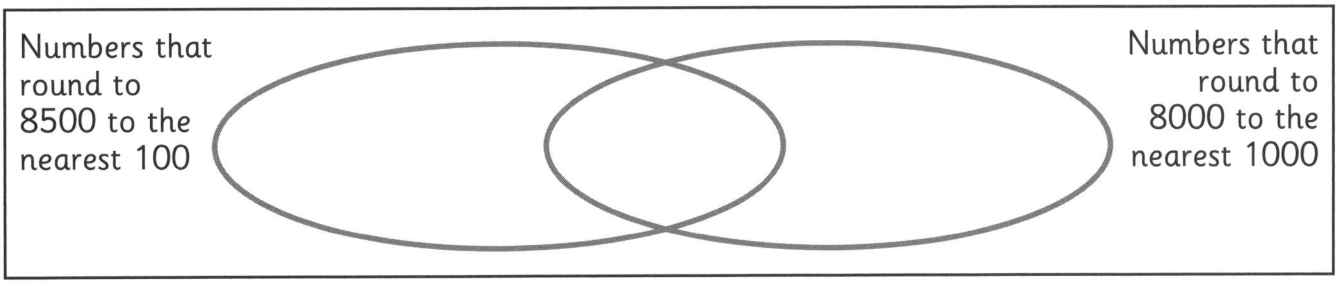

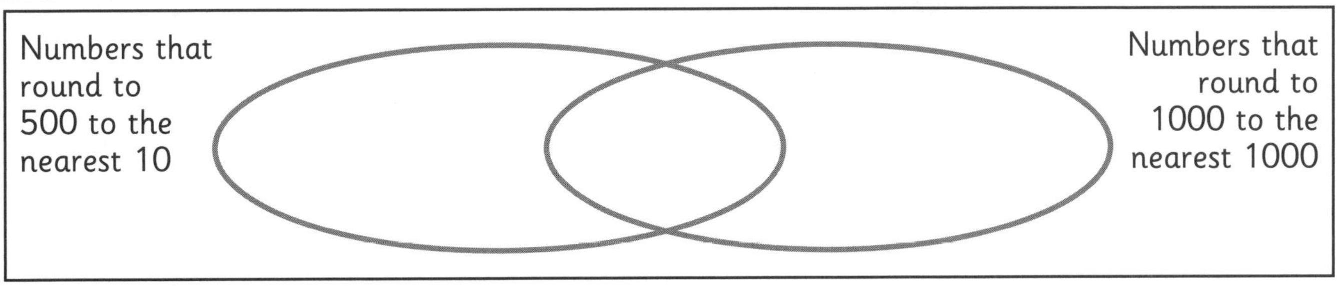

Choose your own labels for the Venn diagram so that you can put numbers in as many sections as possible.

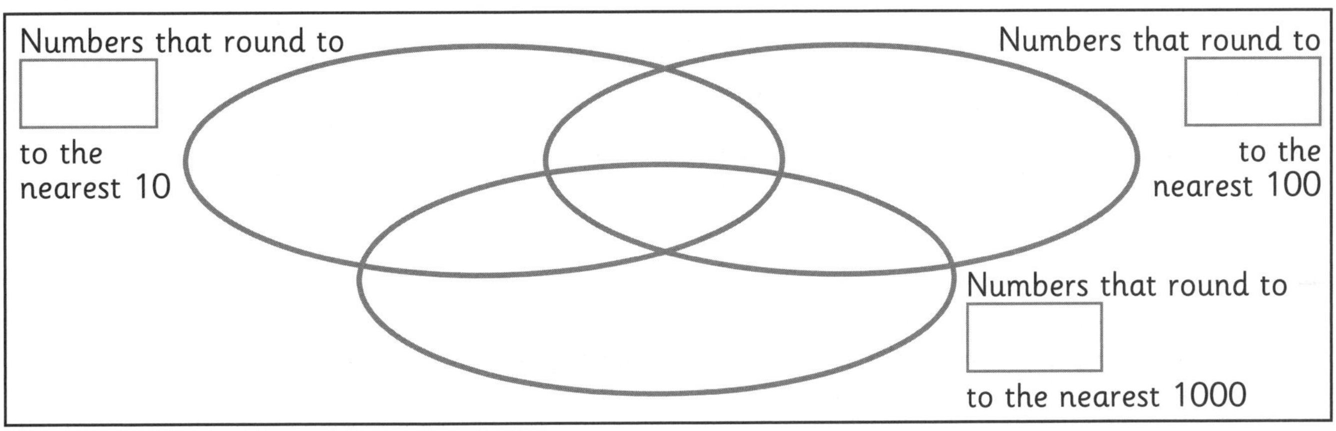

2 There is a fence around a square field.
The farmer measured the fence along one side of the field and found it was 1300 m, to the nearest 100 m.

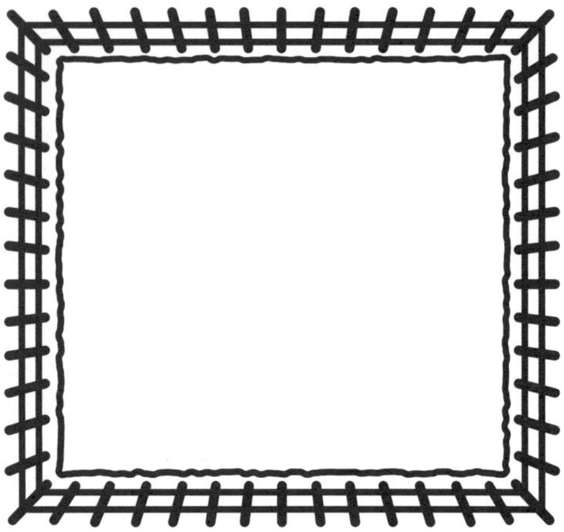

What could be the smallest total perimeter of the field? ____________

What could be the largest total perimeter of the field? ____________

What do you think the total length of the fence must be to the nearest 1000 m?

____

Explain how you got your answer.

____

____

____

3 Rob and Ravi are paid the same each month, except that Rob's money is rounded to the nearest $1000, and Ravi's is rounded to the nearest $100.

After 6 months who had received more money?

Months	January	February	March	April	May	June
Pay ($)	2878	1635	3042	2493	1286	2450

____

Hint: Choose a way to record how much each person gets each month. You could organise the information in a table.

Addition and subtraction

Remember

To solve many of these problems you need to think about whether you will use a mental or written method to add or subtract. Look at the numbers to help you decide which will be most efficient.

Addition and subtraction are the inverse of each other.

Use place value to help you add numbers with decimals.

Vocabulary

addition, subtraction, total, difference

1 Use each digit from 0 to 9 once to make five two-digit numbers.

Find the largest possible total.

Find the smallest possible total.

The largest possible total is __________ .

The smallest possible total is __________ .

Hint: There is more than one way to make the largest and smallest totals.

2 Find a combination of flour bags that totals exactly 1 kg.

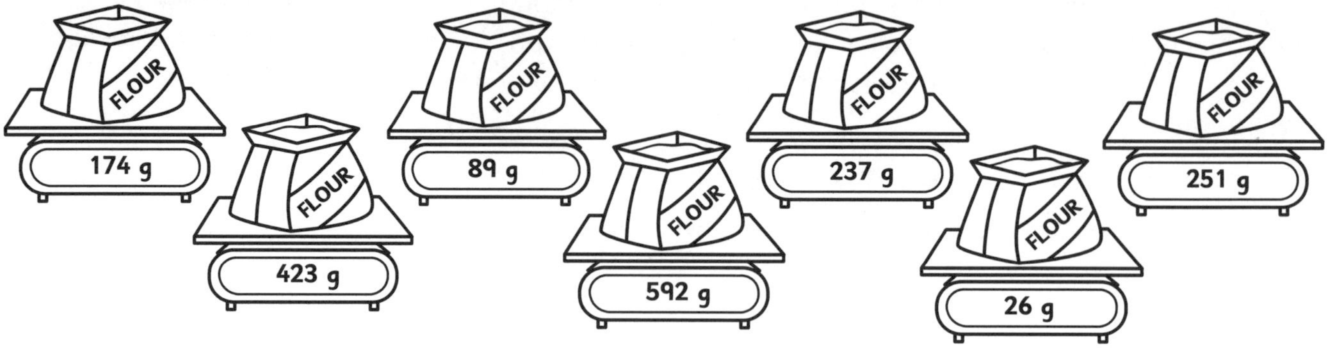

Show your working below.

Hint: You need more than two bags to make 1 kg.
You could first try to find the two bags that cannot go together.
Only one of these bags can be in the solution.

3 What four numbers went into the machine to produce these values?

Hint: You could use the inverse and work backwards.

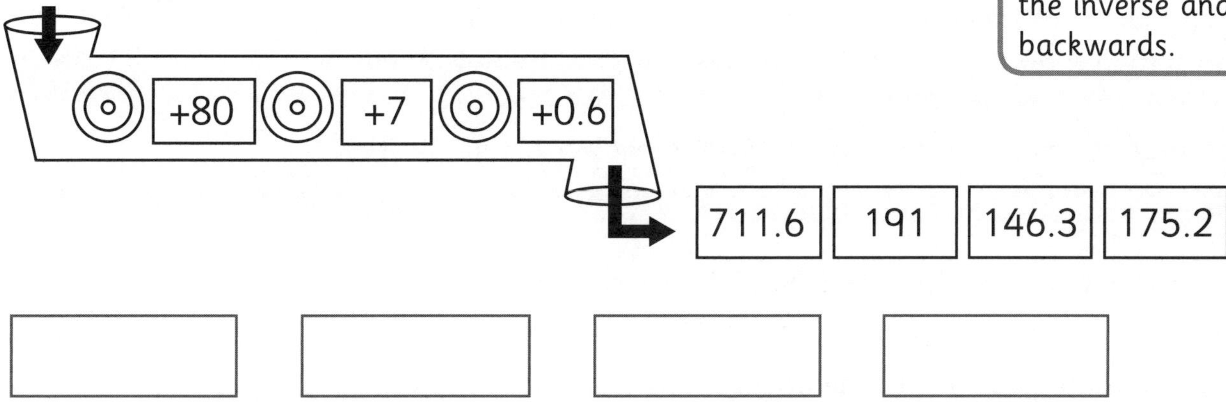

4 Start at the top with 100 m of rope.

Choose your route. Subtract the lengths as you pass through the maze.

You must reach the peg at the bottom with at least 10 m left to climb down.

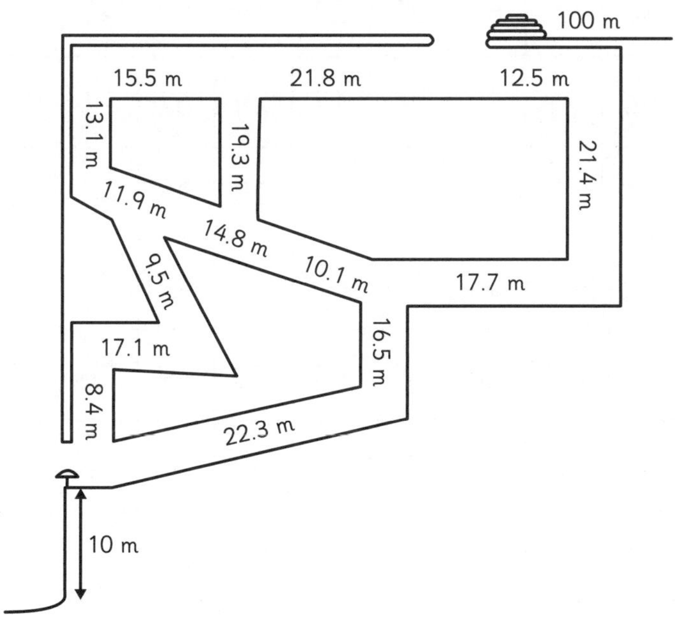

Record your calculations here.

Multiplication and division

Remember

Learning your times tables will help you to solve these problems.
To solve these problems you need to understand that multiplication and division are **inverse** operations.

You can partition numbers and use the grid method for multiplication.

Vocabulary
inverse, operation, product, divisor

1 You can only row to the island through numbers that are multiples of 7.
You can only move horizontally or vertically, not diagonally.

Find the route from one of the boats to the island.

A	63	42	24	65	41	82	63	49	70	14	35	21	7	30	12	53	B
17	36	14	10	16	23	56	28	47	53	24	65	27	70	42	21	49	35
35	70	28	52	7	21	49	41	38	7	63	35	24	14	69	45	27	52
21	62	49	24	70	57	38	14	56	21	39	56	17	29	67	21	70	14
7	41	7	36	28	65	28	49	24	47	52	21	61	28	38	49	22	28
63	17	63	30	21	59	21	68			54	14	60	14	47	70	58	7
49	41	35	56	63	32	35	63			26	49	64	70	29	56	17	63
28	3	60	51	45	39	23	55	27	39	45	70	12	63	7	28	32	49
14	70	56	15	28	42	63	7	21	70	82	42	36	56	27	45	18	70
65	34	24	70	14	16	59	56	38	40	36	28	41	14	28	21	39	56
52	38	61	49	57	43	28	14	51	14	63	7	58	45	73	35	47	21
C	14	63	56	7	21	35	23	70	21	52	35	14	63	42	70	54	D

Hint: Shade the route you try so that you can go back and try different routes.

2 Look at the multiplication grids. Work out the numbers that are being multiplied.

×	?	?
?	3500	280
?	100	8

×	?	?
?	1800	240
?	540	72

×	?	?
?	3200	120
?	480	18

☐ × ☐ = ☐   ☐ × ☐ = ☐   ☐ × ☐ = ☐

Hint: What numbers are being multiplied, to make the products in the grids?

3 6 children are doing crafts and making collages. They share the materials equally.

95 ribbons

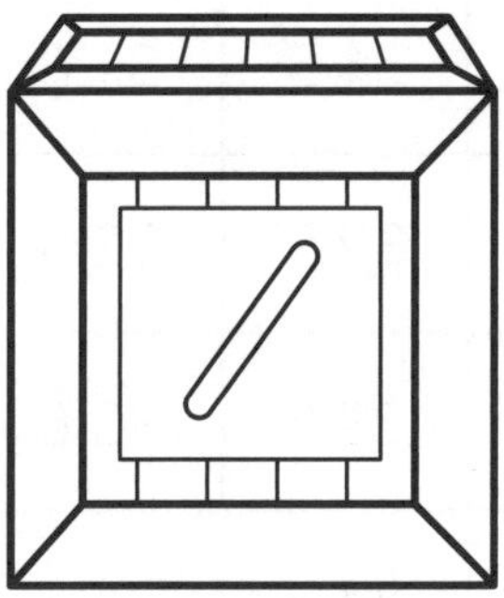

139 lolly sticks

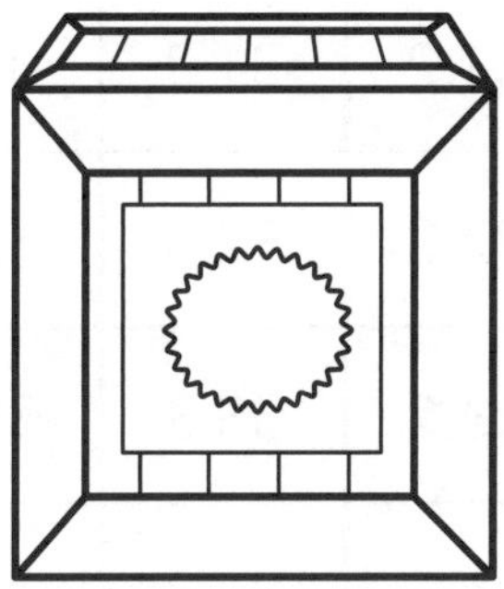

158 pom poms

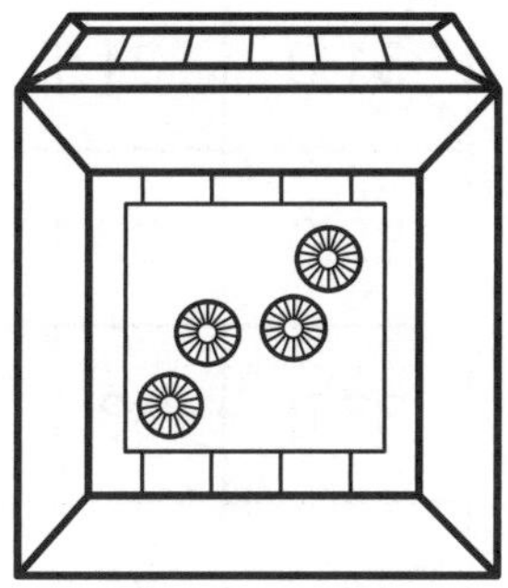

172 sequins

How many of each item do they get?

☐ ribbons each

☐ lolly sticks each

☐ pom poms each

☐ sequins each

How many are left over in the box?

☐ ribbons left

☐ lolly sticks left

☐ pom poms left

☐ sequins left

Discuss with your partner the methods you use. Check each other's answers.

4 Work out the missing numbers in the calculations.

1 × ☐ = 33.6	2 × ☐ = 71.6	10 × ☐ = 348
2 × ☐ = 65.6	3 × ☐ = 99.9	2 × ☐ = 70.6
10 × ☐ = 334	3 × ☐ = 96.3	2 × ☐ = 64.6
5 × ☐ = 171.5	4 × ☐ = 132.4	6 × ☐ = 202.8
7 × ☐ = 217.7	8 × ☐ = 254.4	9 × ☐ = 298.8

Shade them on the grid below to reveal a number.

30.0	30.1	30.2	30.3	30.4	30.5	30.6	30.7	30.8	30.9
31.0	31.1	31.2	31.3	31.4	31.5	31.6	31.7	31.8	31.9
32.0	32.1	32.2	32.3	32.4	32.5	32.6	32.7	32.8	32.9
33.0	33.1	33.2	33.3	33.4	33.5	33.6	33.7	33.8	33.9
34.0	34.1	34.2	34.3	34.4	34.5	34.6	34.7	34.8	34.9
35.0	35.1	35.2	35.3	35.4	35.5	35.6	35.7	35.8	35.9

Hint: Multiplying by 2 is the same as doubling and dividing by 2 is the same as halving.
Use place value to multiply or divide by 10.
All of the answers are in the grid.

Multiples, square numbers and factors

Remember

A **square number** is the product made by multiplying a whole number by itself.

To solve these problems you need to know how to test whether a number is a **factor** of another number.

Vocabulary

square number, divisible, test of divisibility, factor

1 Put these numbers into the Venn diagram.

785 1040 998 48 330 7585 48 021

31 970 72 132 60 075 59 927 4294 8599

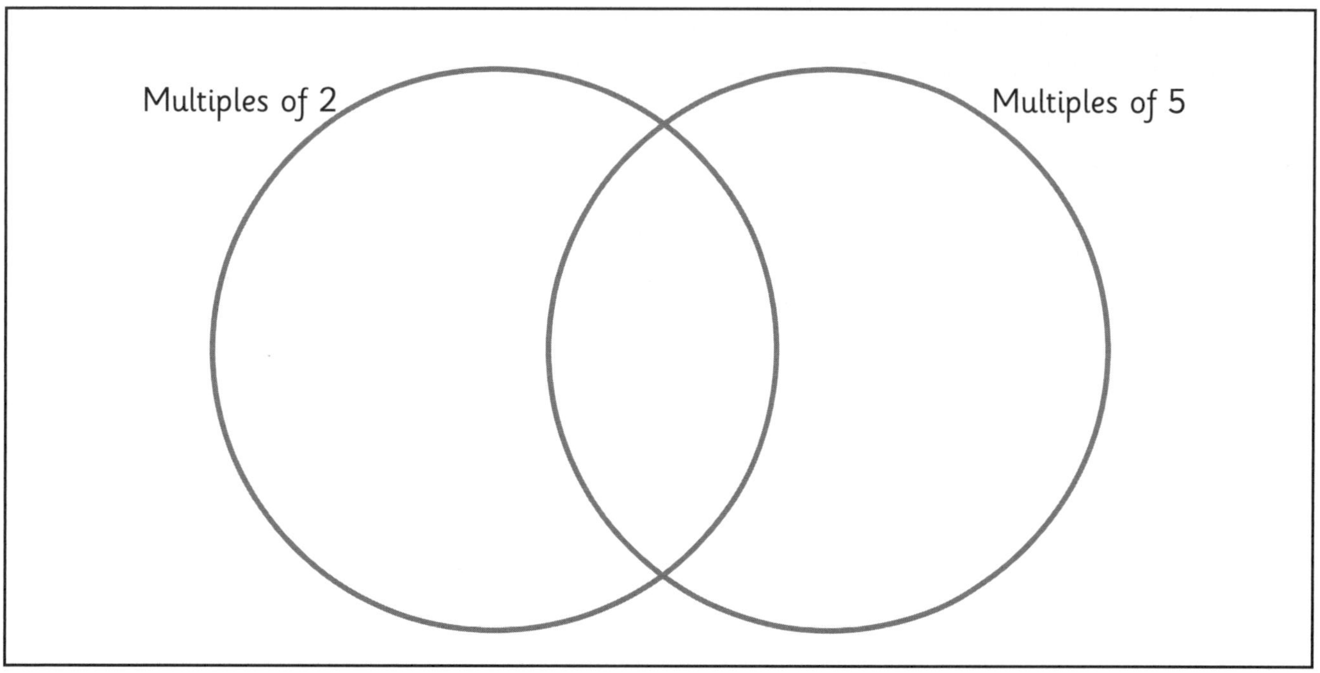

Describe the numbers in the overlapping section of the diagram.

____

Hint: Use your tests of divisibility for multiples of 2 and 5.

2 9 is a square number.

16 is a square number.

9 + 16 = 25. 25 is a square number.

It is possible to find a total that is a square number by adding four different square numbers under 100?

Use this space to investigate.

☐ + ☐ + ☐ + ☐ = ☐

Hint: Write down the square numbers to 100.
Work systematically to add the numbers together.

3 Which number in this grid has the most factors?

61	62	63	64	65	66	67	68	69	70
71	72	73	74	75	76	77	78	79	80

Use this space to investigate.

Hint: Find pairs of factors systematically, for example, is the number a multiple of 2? If it is, what is 2 multiplied by to make the number? Is the number a multiple of 3? If it is, then what is 3 multiplied by to make the number?

Parallel, perpendicular and cuboids

Remember
Parallel lines are always the same distance apart.
Perpendicular lines meet or cross at 90°.
A **cuboid** has six faces. Opposite faces on a cuboid are the same length and width.

You will need: thick paper/thin card, ruler, scissors, sticky tape, colouring pen

Vocabulary
parallel, perpendicular, right angle, cuboid, cube, net

1 This is an octagon with two pairs of parallel sides.

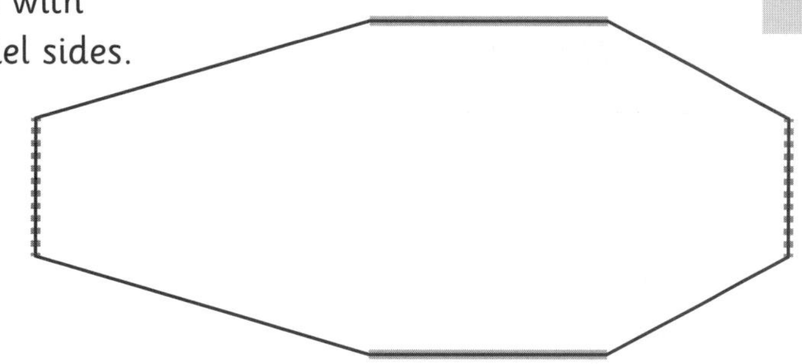

Draw each of these shapes. Mark the pairs of parallel sides with a coloured pen.

A pentagon with one pair of parallel sides

Hint: You could sketch the shape first, without using a ruler, to help you to visualise it. Then draw it with a ruler to space the parallel sides accurately. The parallel lines do not need to be the same length as each other.

A hexagon with three pairs of parallel sides

A heptagon with two pairs of parallel sides

2 Measure and copy this net carefully onto thick paper or thin card. Check that the lines meeting at the corners are perpendicular and the opposite sides are parallel.

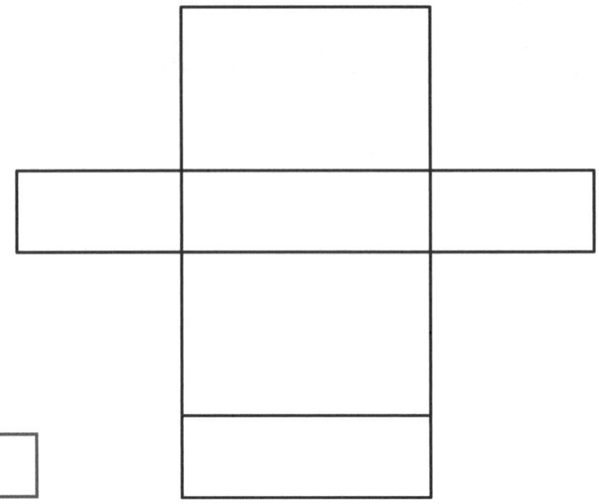

Fold the net to make the cuboid.

Measure the lengths of the sides of the cuboid to the nearest centimetre.

Length = ______ Width = ______ Height = ______

Draw the nets and make three more cuboids so that all four will stack underneath like this …

and fit inside each other like this.

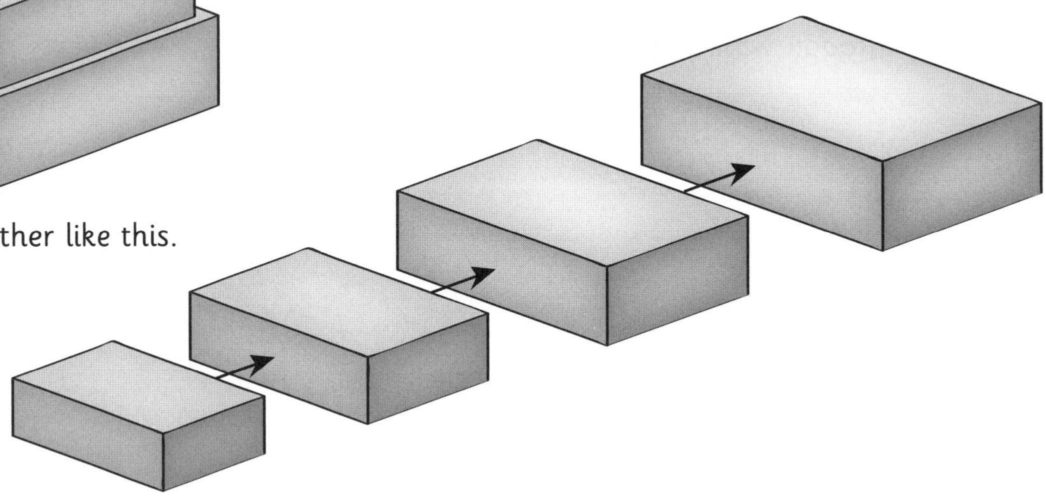

Write the measurements of your cuboids.

Second cuboid	**Third cuboid**	**Fourth cuboid**
Length = ______	Length = ______	Length = ______
Width = ______	Width = ______	Width = ______
Height = ______	Height = ______	Height = ______

Hint: Use a right-angle checker to check that lines are perpendicular to each other. Use a ruler to check that lines are parallel.

Mass

Remember

To solve these problems you need to be able to read a scale accurately. Work out what each unlabelled division mark on the scale stands for and remember to use the correct units for mass.

1000 g = 1 kg
100 g = 0.1 kg
10 g = 0.01 kg
1 g = 0.001 kg

You will need:
weighing scales, sand, bags, spoon, ruler, labels

Vocabulary
mass, gram, kilogram

1 Make bags of sand that have a mass of:

1 kg, 100 g, 0.4 kg, 20 g, 0.25 kg, 0.09 kg, 0.9 kg, 865 g

Estimate the amount of sand you put in the bag first, then place each sand bag on the weighing scales and adjust the amount of sand until it has the correct mass.

Make labels showing each measured mass. Challenge a partner to match your labels to the sand bags you have made.

Put the sand bags and labels in order, from least to greatest mass.

Draw or stick a photograph of your sand bags here.

Hint: Your measurements will need to be as accurate as you can make them for the other person to match the correct labels to the bags. Convert all the measurements to kilograms or grams to check they are in the correct order.

2 The same parcel is placed on each of the weighing scales below.
Draw the needle on scales A–D to show the mass.

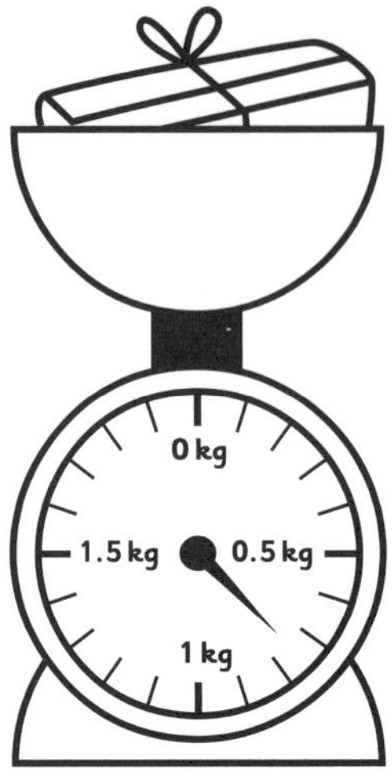

A

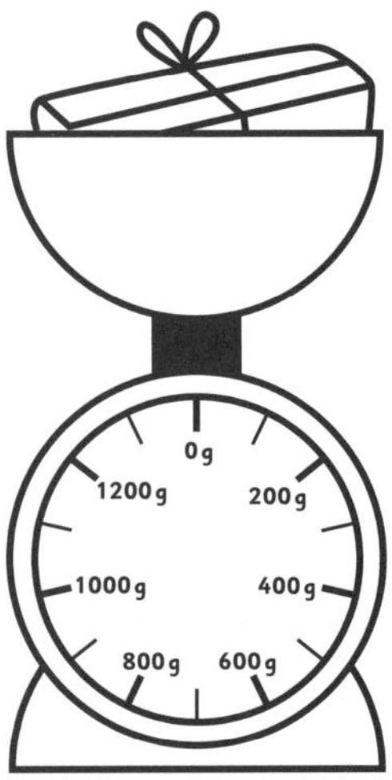

B

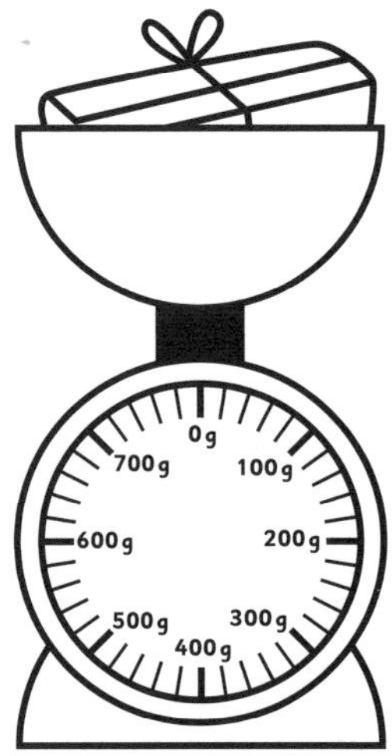

C

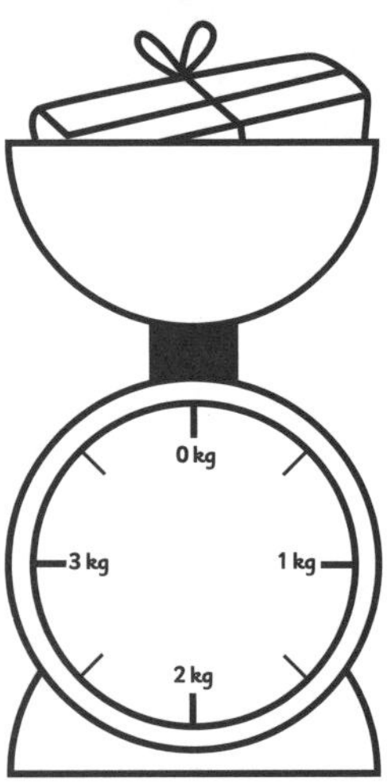

D

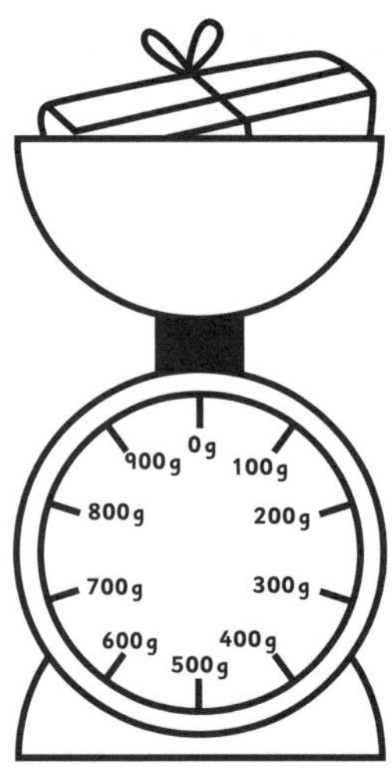

Hint: Work out the mass of the parcel on the first weighing scales in both kilograms and grams.
Use a ruler to draw the needles on the scales.

Numbers and sequences

Remember

You can draw a number line with numbers above and below 0 to order and compare negative and positive numbers.

odd × odd = odd   odd × even = even   even × even = even

Vocabulary

consecutive numbers, sequence, general statement, positive, negative

1 Each of these children has recorded the temperature where they live.

Huda: 32°C   Sunita: 28°C   Gerel: –9°C

Julieta: –2°C   Abigail: 13°C   Isla: –12°C

Write the temperatures in order from lowest to highest.

☐, ☐, ☐, ☐, ☐, ☐

Mark the temperature of each child's location on this thermometer. Huda's is done for you.

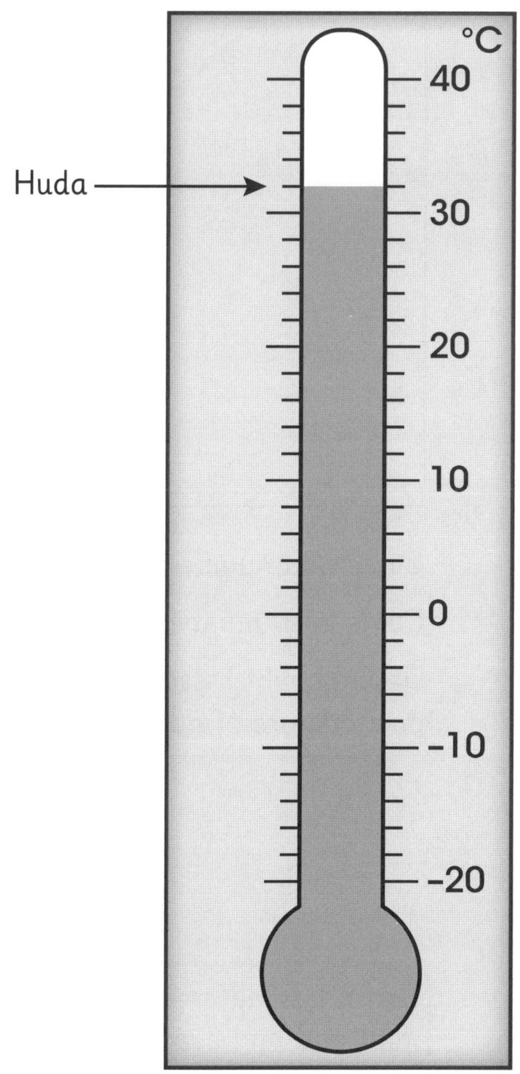

What is the difference between Huda's and Gerel's temperatures?

☐ degrees

How much warmer is Julieta compared to Isla?

☐ degrees

How much colder is Julieta compared to Sunita?

☐ degrees

Which two children have a difference of 25°?

☐ and ☐

2 Write one number between 0 and 500 in each space in the Venn diagram.

Write one number between 500 and 1000 in each space in the Venn diagram.

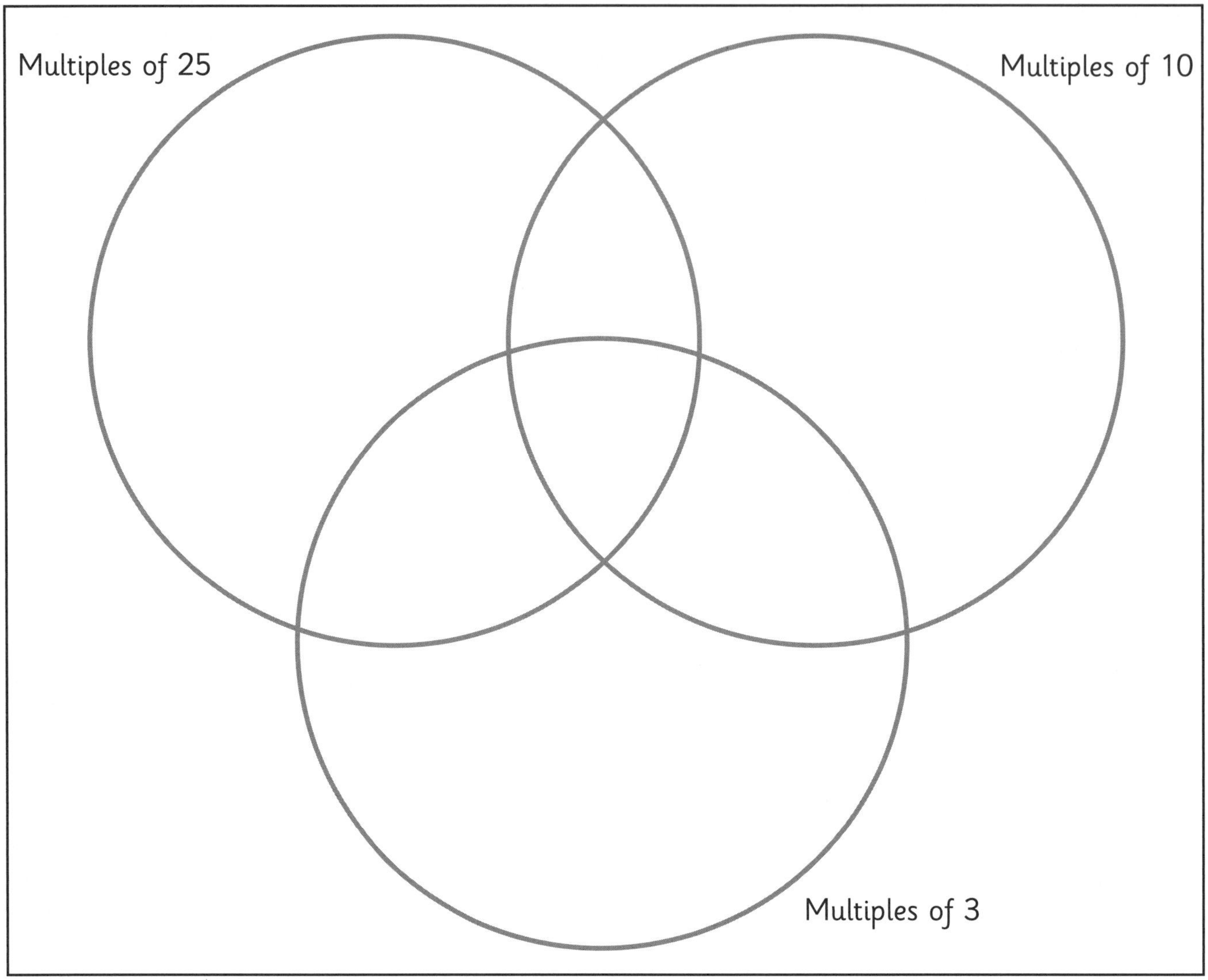

Circle odd numbers on the Venn diagram in blue.

Circle even numbers on the Venn diagram in red.

Describe which sections have all even numbers, all odd numbers, or a mixture of odd and even numbers.

Hint: Use different numbers to check whether it is possible to find odd and even numbers for each section of the diagram.

3 Complete these number patterns.

A ____, 57, 46, 35, 24, ____, ____, ____, ____, ____

B ____, ____, ____, –17, –9, –1, ____, ____, ____, ____

C 102, ____, 72, ____, 42, ____, 12, ____, –18, ____

Hint: You could use a number line to help work out the numbers below zero.

4 Fahad and Jamal are playing a game.

They spin the two spinners.

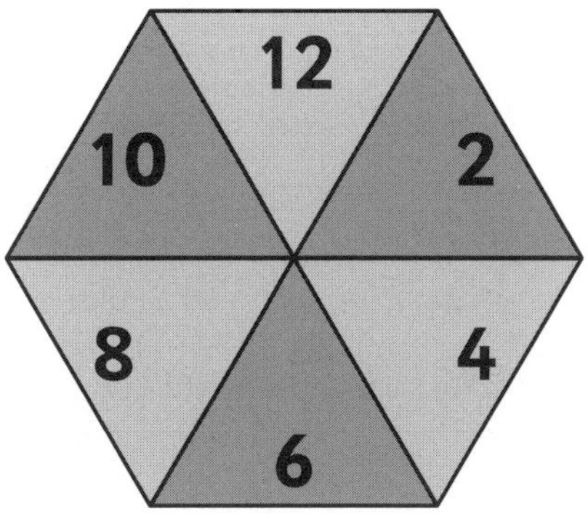

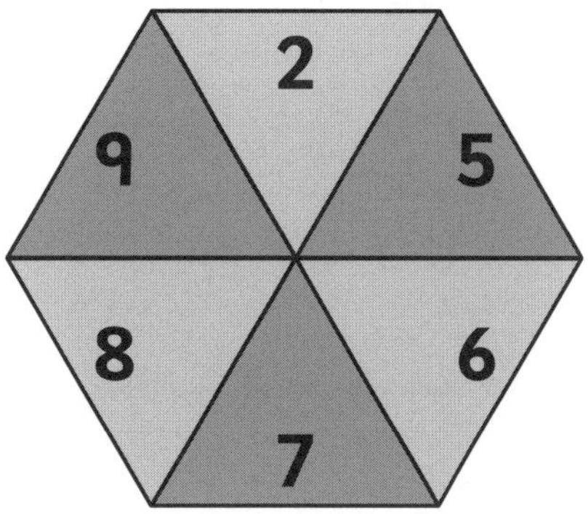

If the product of the two numbers shown on the spinners is even, Fahad takes a counter.

If the product is odd, Jamal takes a counter.

The winner is the person with more counters after 10 spins.

Who will win? ____

Why?

Hint: Try playing the game with a partner.
Try to explain to each other what happens.

Decimals

Remember
To solve these problems you need to understand that the position of a digit in a number is important to its value. Some of the positions are hundreds, tens, ones, tenths and hundredths. It can be useful to refer to a place-value chart. Numbers with decimals can be rounded to the nearest whole number. If a number is halfway between two other numbers then always round up.

You will need:
place-value chart (optional)

Vocabulary
tenth, hundredth

1 Complete the magic square with these numbers so that every vertical, horizontal and diagonal adds up to 1.5.

0.1 0.2 0.3 0.4 0.6 0.7 0.8 0.9

Use each number only once.

	0.5	

2 Write down all of the numbers that can be made using these four cards. You must use each card just once in each number.

9 **5** **1** **•**

Choose five of your numbers to complete this statement.

	<		<		<		<	

Now choose five of your numbers to complete this statement.

	>		>		>		>	

3 Draw lines to join the pairs of numbers that total 10.

2.05	9.3	5.25	4.3	8.48
6.17	5.7	6.38	3.83	0.06
3.3	6.27	7.95	0.7	6.7
3.62	1.52	8.88	7.59	9.94
7.78	3.73	2.41	2.22	4.75

Double the extra number in the grid. ☐

Hint: Find the pairs with one decimal place first.

4 Choose a number in the grid.

Halve the number.

If the halved number rounds to a multiple of 7, shade the square.

Continue until a number is revealed.

53.4	13.1	55.62	140.16
100.18	12.98	67.22	98.56
142.34	29.5	111.34	42.4
110.56	43.08	124.3	28.96
85.46	69.18	125.02	84.7

Hint: You can check whether your halving is correct by doubling the number. Doubling is the inverse of halving.

5 Find two pairs of numbers in the grid in activity 4 that total to make a whole number.

Addition, subtraction, multiplication and division

Remember

Learning your times tables will help you to solve some of these problems.

To solve these problems you need to choose appropriate mental or written methods of addition, subtraction, multiplication and division. Think about the different strategies you have learned and try to choose the best ones for each problem

Vocabulary

difference, product, total, remainder

1 Each box needs two keys.

The number on the box is the total made by the two keys.

Work out the number for the last box.

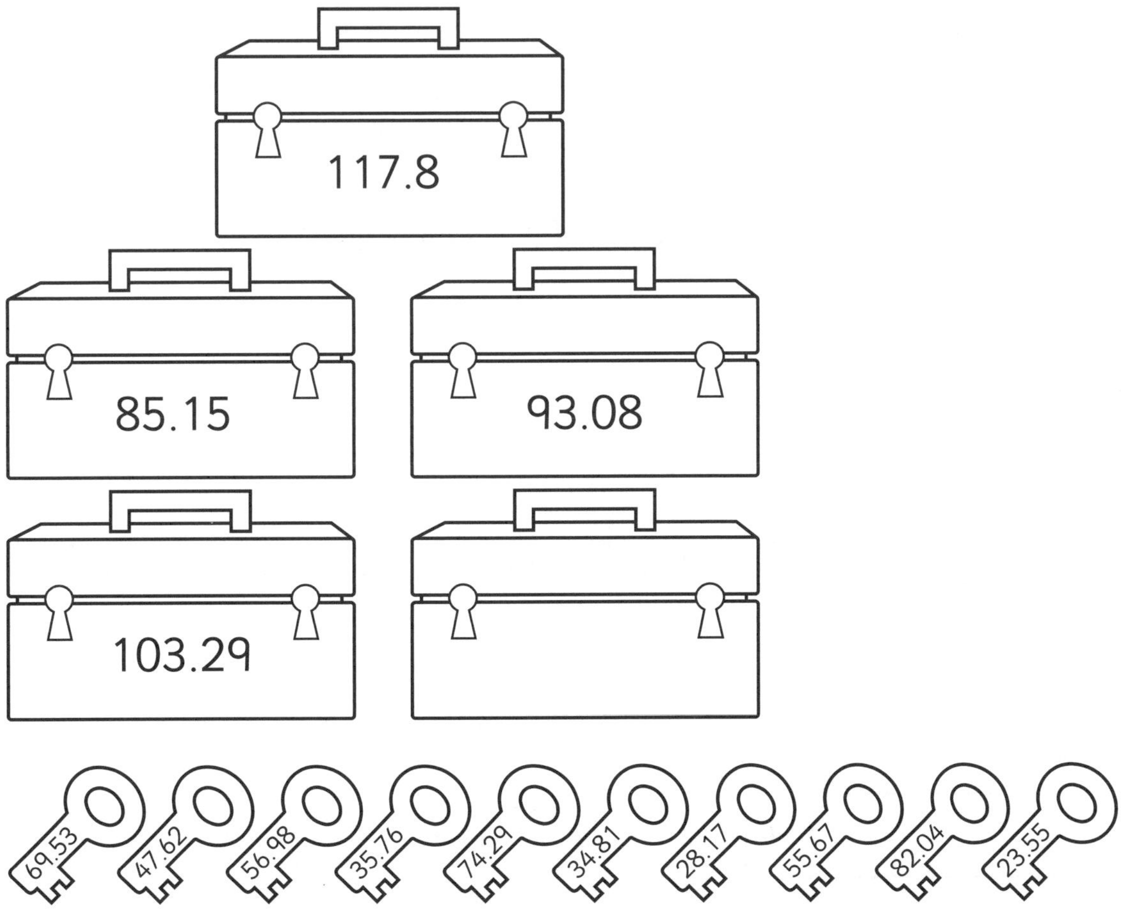

Hint: Work systematically. Each key has a partner to open one of the locks.

2 Play this game with a partner or adult.

Spin the spinner eight times. Each time, both players write the number on the spinner in one of their boxes.

When all of the boxes are filled, players complete the calculation they have made.

The player with the higher answer wins.

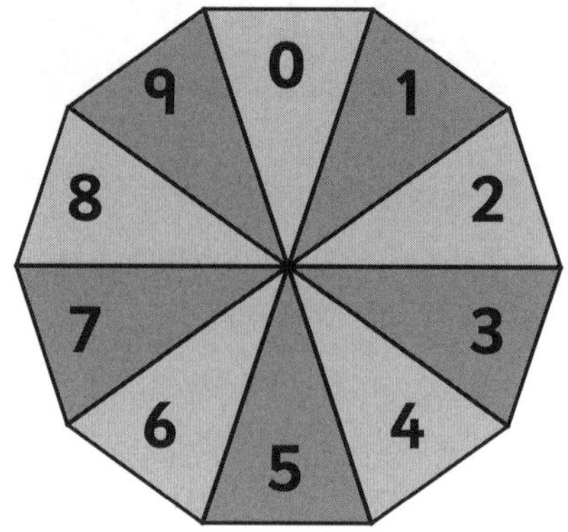

Player 1 □□□
× □
\+ □□□□ = ______

Player 2 □□□
× □
\+ □□□□ = ______

Consider how you could improve you method of playing the game.

Play again.

Player 1 □□□
× □
\+ □□□□ = ______

Player 2 □□□
× □
\+ □□□□ = ______

Hint: Use jottings or written calculation methods to solve the multiplication and addition. Think about how place value changes the result.

3 Shade the numbers on the grid that leave a remainder of 4 when divided by 8.

Example: 116 ÷ 8 = 14 remainder 4.

100	101	102	103	104	105	106	107	108	109
110	111	112	113	114	115	116	117	118	119
120	121	122	123	124	125	126	127	128	129
130	131	132	133	134	135	136	137	138	139
140	141	142	143	144	145	146	147	148	149

Hint: Once you have found some numbers that leave a remainder of 4, look for a pattern to predict the next number.
You could use a written method to find the total.

Describe the properties of the shaded numbers.

Find the total of the shaded numbers.

4 Which pair of these numbers has a difference closest to 700?

269, 403, 989, 1098, 1578, 2099, 2297, 2811

☐ − ☐ = ☐

Hint: The numbers are all near multiples of 10 or 100.

5 Investigate whether this is true.

Record your investigation here.

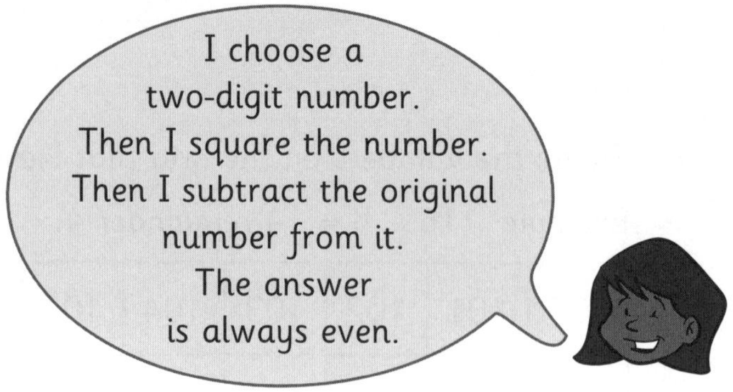

Use what you know about products of even and odd numbers to explain your results.

Hint: Squaring a number means multiplying it by itself, for example,
17 squared = 17 × 17 = 289.
Make sure you try both odd and even starting numbers.

Questions, surveys, data and finding the mode

Remember

When drawing a graph choose a scale that allows you to represent the data accurately, but do not label so many divisions that the scale becomes cluttered.

Use a ruler to draw graphs. Label your graphs. You need a title and axes labels.

The **mode** of a set of data is the category that occurs the most.

You will need: a ruler

Vocabulary
hypothesis, data,
data collection sheet,
prediction, frequency,
frequency table,
bar line graph, mode, modal

1 You have been asked to find out what children would like organised for a school picnic.

What three questions would you ask children?

Data collection sheet

1.

2.

3.

Talk with a partner about your questions and why you chose them.

Hint: A data collection sheet can offer a list of choices, for example:
Which activity would you prefer?
rounders ☐ scavenger hunt ☐ singing ☐

2 Draw a bar line graph to represent the data in the frequency table. Choose the best vertical scale for the data considering the effect of changing the scale on the vertical axis.

Remember to label the axes and give your graph a title.

> **Hint:** Your scale could go up in 2s, 5s, 10s, 20s or 100s.

How many hours of sleep do you get in one night? Answer to the nearest hour.

Hours of sleep	Number of people	Hours of sleep	Number of people
6	|	10	卌 卌 卌 卌 卌 |||
7	卌 ||||	11	卌 卌 卌 ||
8	卌 卌 卌	12	||||
9	卌 卌 卌 卌 |||		

How many people are represented in the frequency table? [ ]

What is the mode for this data? [ ]

Write three questions that could be answered from the graph.

Then give the answers.

1. ______________________________

Answer: ______________

2. ______________________________

Answer: ______________

3. ______________________________

Answer: ______________

Line graphs

Remember
To draw a line graph, plot the points that are provided then draw a line with a ruler between the points.

Use a line graph only when the intermediate points have meaning.

You will need: a ruler

Vocabulary
line graph, intermediate points

1 Some children planted a stick in the ground.

They measured the length of its shadow six times in one day and drew a line graph of their results.

This is what the children said about the graph they made.

"At 9am the length of the shadow was 21 cm."

"The shadow was shortest at 12 o'clock."

"The difference between the longest and shortest measurements was 15.5 cm."

"The longest measurement was taken in the morning."

"The difference in length between 10 a.m. and 11 a.m. was 5.5 cm."

"The shadow gradually got shorter in the morning, then longer again in the afternoon."

"The measurement at 11 a.m. was a square number."

"The measurement at 2 p.m. was 8 cm longer than the shortest measurement."

"The shadow at 1 pm was $\frac{1}{2}$ cm shorter than it had been at 11 a.m."

Use the information to draw their line graph.

Remember to label the axes and give the graph a title.

Use your graph to estimate how long the shadow was at half past 1. ☐

Hint: Draw a table of times and shadow lengths, to start working out points on the graph. Remember to label your axes.

2 Use the information in the tables to complete the two line graphs.

Freezing sugary water	
Time (minutes)	**Temperature (°C)**
0	12
10	8
20	4
30	1
40	–2
50	–4
60	–5

Freezing salty water	
Time (minutes)	**Temperature (°C)**
0	12
10	7
20	3
30	–1
40	–4
50	–6
60	–7

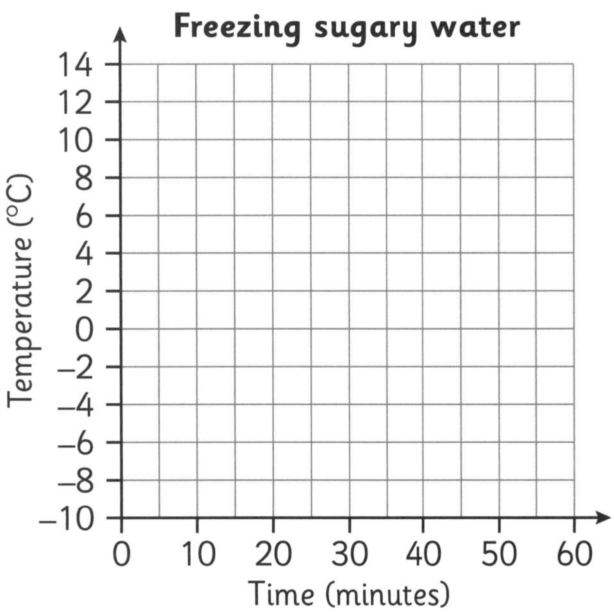

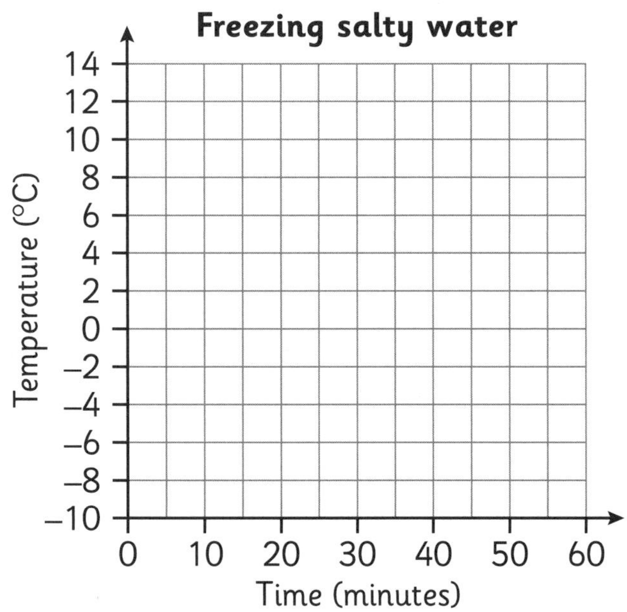

Write three sentences comparing how the sugary and salty water froze.

Why is a line graph a good choice for displaying this data?

Hint: Compare the temperatures of the salty and sugary water by looking at the same times on each graph.

Probability

Remember
To solve these problems you need to understand the vocabulary of chance and probability.

A probability line can be used to record the chance of something happening, from impossible or no chance, to certain.

You will need:
coloured pencils or pens

Vocabulary
probability, likelihood, chance, fair/unfair, probability line

1 Colour spinner A to make these probability statements true.

There is no chance of spinning red.

There is a poor chance of spinning yellow.

Spinning blue is likely.

It is unlikely that the spinner will land on green.

It is impossible to spin purple.

A

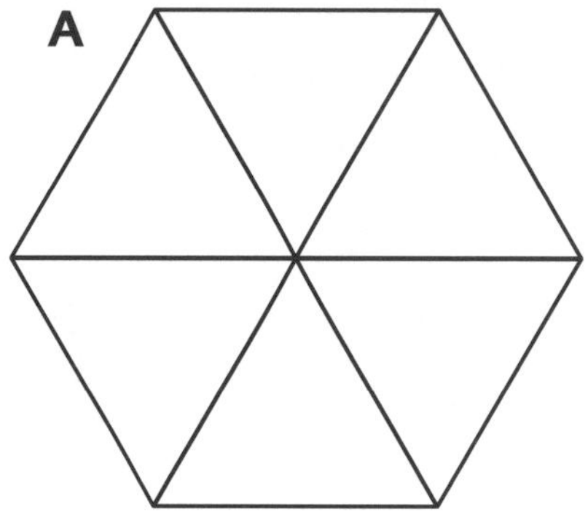

Now colour spinner B.
Use the same probability statements.

B

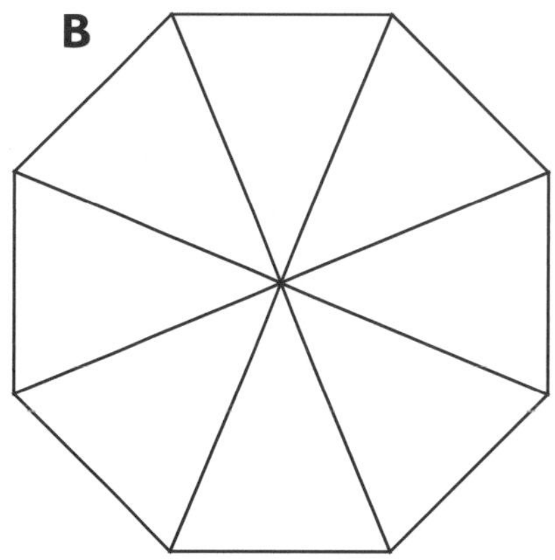

Which spinner has the greater probability of spinning blue? A / B

Which spinner has the smaller probability of spinning yellow? A / B

Hint: Compare the size of the fractions shaded on the two spinners to see which has the greater probability of each colour.

2 This is the net of a six-sided dice.

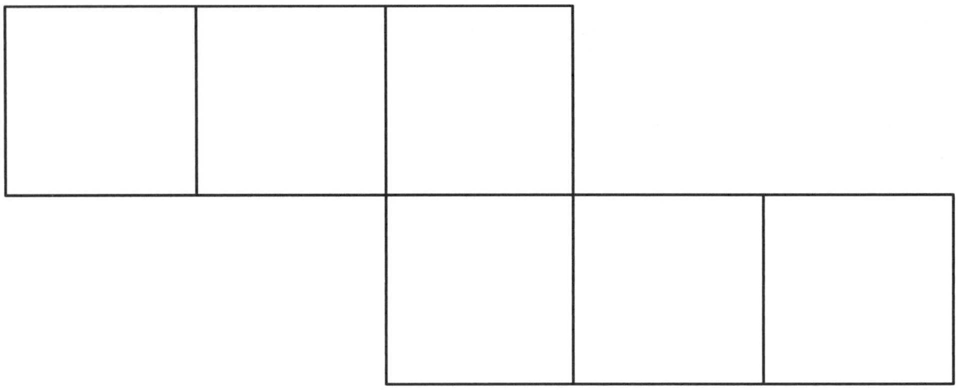

Number the dice so that:

There is an even chance of throwing a number greater than 5.

It is likely that the number thrown will be even.

It is impossible to throw a multiple of 3.

Throwing a number less than 0 is unlikely.

For your dice write a new statement on each box of the probability scale.

certain

good chance

even chance

poor chance

no chance

Hint: Example: If a number greater than 50 has no chance of being rolled on your dice, you could write that in the box next to 'no chance'.

3 Some children have been investigating probability.

They are taking shapes out of bags without looking.

Draw a line from each child to a bag.

One of these bags of shapes does not belong to any of the children.

Complete the statements for this extra bag of shapes.

The probability of taking a prism from the bag is ☐.

The probability of taking a 3D shape from the bag is ☐.

The probability of taking a pyramid from the bag is ☐.

Hint: Remember that cubes and cuboids are types of prism.

Length

Remember
To measure with a ruler make sure that the start of the line or object lines up with the 0 position on the ruler.

1 m = 100 cm = 1000 mm

You will need: a ruler

Vocabulary
metre, centimetre, millimetre

1 Measure each of these plants to the nearest millimetre.

Plot the height of the plants on the graph. Join the points to make a line graph.

Use the information from the line graph to draw a plant to match what the height might have been on day 4.

Label the height of the plant.

Unit 2C: Measure and problem solving
CPM framework 5Dh3, 5Ml1, 5Ml2, 5Ml3, 5Ml4. 5Ml5, 5Ml7, 5Ps1, 5Pt1; Teacher's Resource 19.1

Height of plant

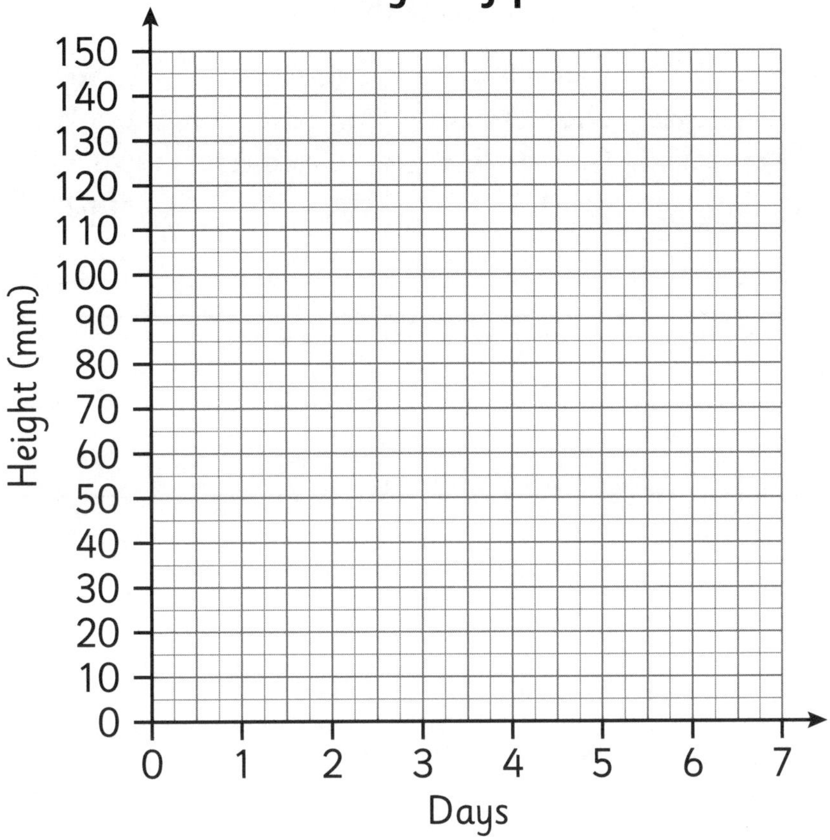

Day 4 =

2 The depth of each of these holes has been measured and recorded.
The measurements have been muddled up.

Match the measurements to the holes.

1.68 m   2.3 m   109 cm   1.9 m   234 cm   180 cm

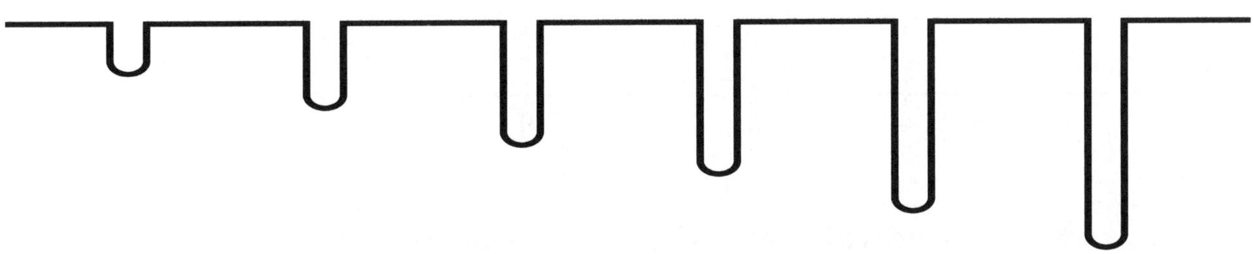

Depth =	Depth =	Depth =	Depth =	Depth =	Depth =

Hint: You will need to order the measurements. To order them you should convert some of the measurements so that they are all in metres, or all in centimetres.

3 Plot the corners of the triangles onto the grid and complete the table.

Triangle	Coordinates	Length of shortest side (to nearest cm)	Length of shortest side (to nearest mm)	Length of longest side (to nearest cm)	Length of longest side (to nearest mm)
A	(2, 1), (2, 3), (5, 1)				
B	(8, 3), (5, 7), (8, 7)				
C	(1, 5), (3, 3), (3, 8)				

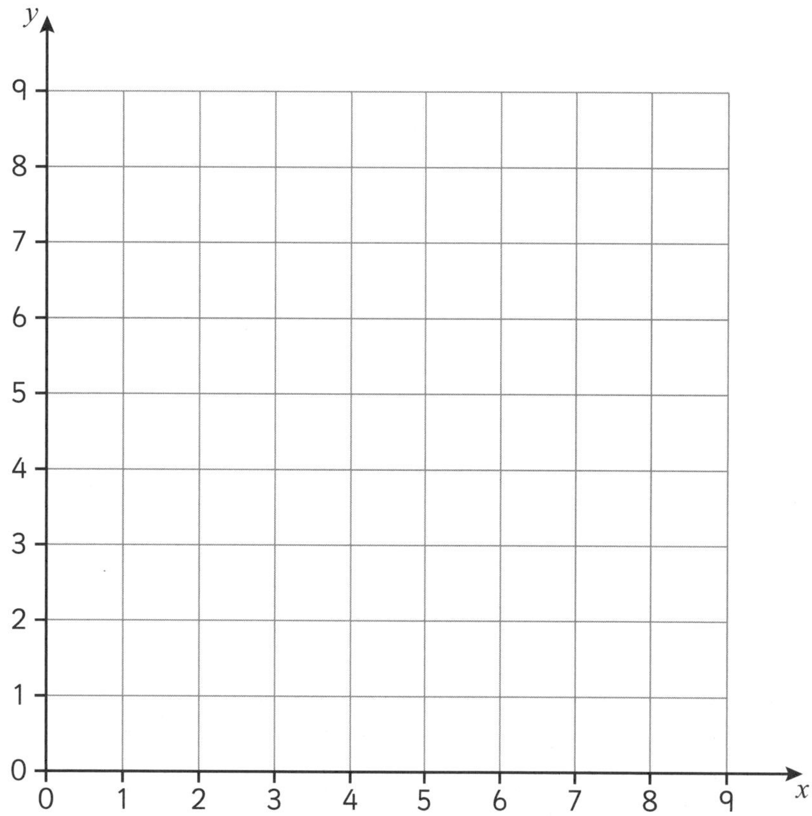

Hint: Check that all measurements and units are reasonable.

Time

Remember

To solve these problems you need to understand the units used for time, including years, months, weeks, days, hours, minutes and seconds.

You can draw a time line and use it like a number line to work out time intervals.

You will need: calendar, bus or train timetable, ruler

Vocabulary

12-hour clock, 24-hour clock, analogue, digital

1 Make your own timetable. Use 24-hour clock times.

There are four stops on the bus route. You can name the stops.

There are two buses. They can go back and forth along the route as many times as you like.

These are the times between stops.

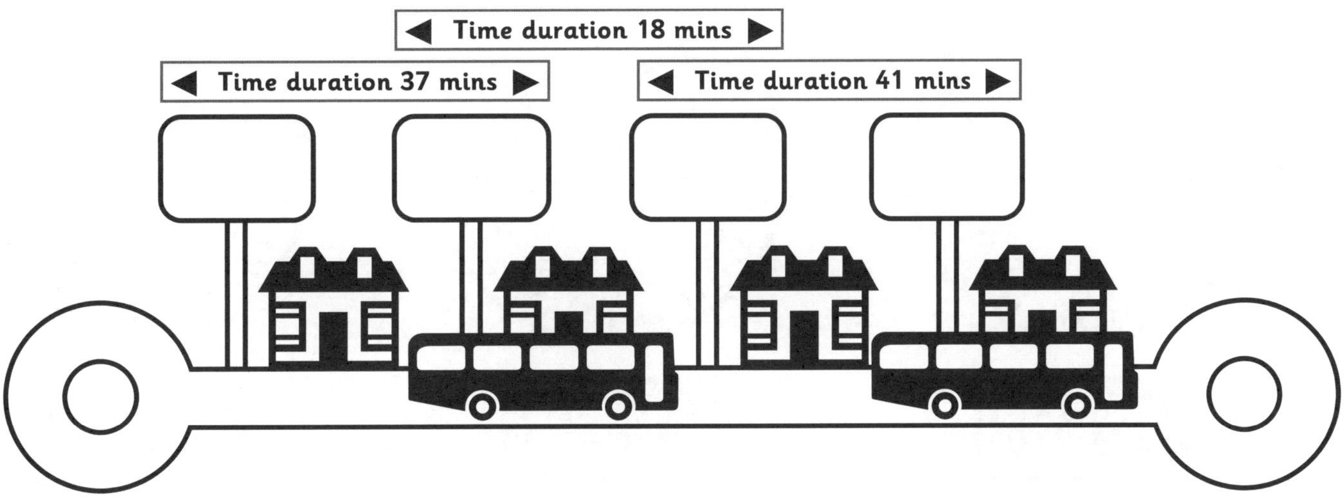

From ______ to ______ :

From ______ to ______ :

Hint: Look at other bus or train timetables for ideas. Write the journey times from the first stop to the fourth stop in the first table. Write the return journey times from the fourth stop to the first stop in the second table.

2 Draw the hands on the clocks to show the times as accurately as possible.

19:06

00:24

14:48

09:42

07:03

17:39

Hint: Use a ruler to draw the hands. Think about how many minutes are represented by one interval on the clock scale for the hour hand.

3 The first spacecraft to journey from Earth to Mars was NASA's Mariner 4. It launched on 28th November 1964 and arrived at Mars on 14th July 1965.

How long did the journey take? ____________________

Mariner 6, launched on 25th February 1969 and arrived on Mars on 31st July 1969.

Mariner 9 launched on 30th May 1971, and arrived on 13th November 1971.

Which flight was quicker? ____________________

What is the difference in time taken between the two flights? ____________________

Hint: Choose whether to calculate the journey in days, weeks, months or years.

4 Today is the 20th day of the month and it is a Monday.

On which day of the week could the 20th day be next month?

____

____

____

____

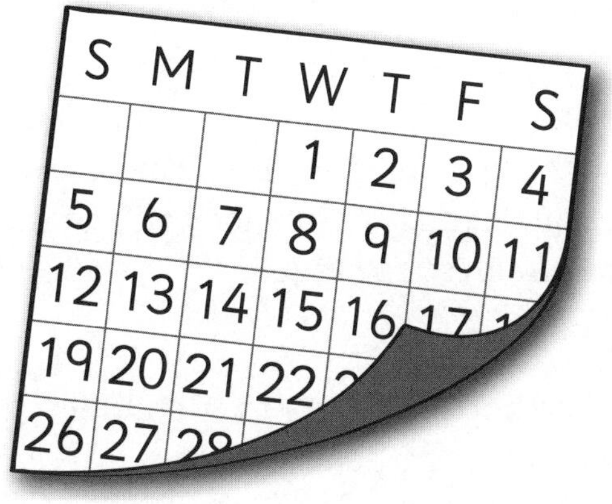

Hint: Remember how many days there are in each month. Use a calendar to solve this problem.

5 The 12th day of next month will be on a Monday.

What is this month?

List the possible years in the 21st century that this calendar could be for.

____

____

____

____

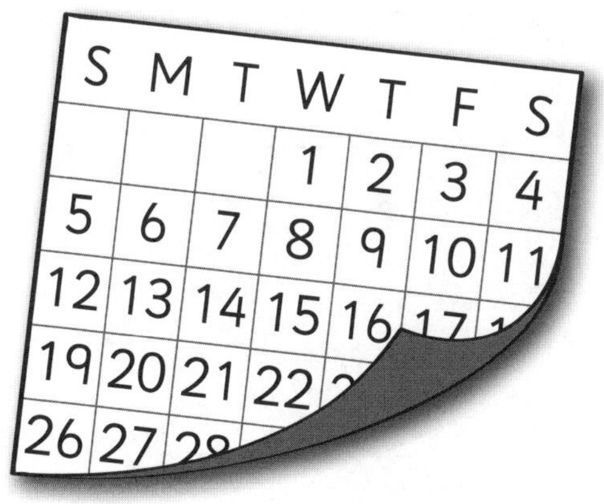

Mental strategies

Remember
You know lots of strategies to calculate with numbers quickly in your head. Always look at the numbers carefully and choose the best strategy.

Strategies include:

Round one or both numbers to a multiple of 10, 100 or 1000, calculate, then adjust for the difference.
Use factors to multiply, for example, $7 \times 90 = 7 \times 9 \times 10$, and $15 \times 6 = 15 \times 2 \times 3$

You will need: 20 counters

Vocabulary
difference, product, sum, total

1 This is a game for two players.

Spin both spinners.

The first player to say the correct product of the two numbers on the spinners wins a counter.

The player with more counters after 20 spins is the winner.

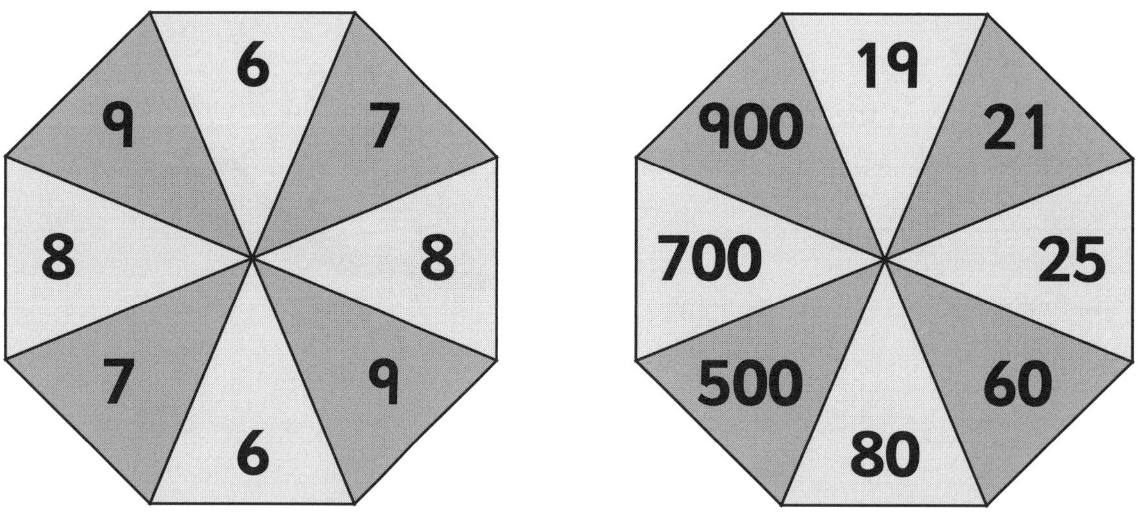

Hint: Use mental calculation strategies, such as rounding or multiplying by factors.

2 Choose a number.

3997 **5011** **4006**

4988 **4998**

Find the difference between your number and the number at the top of the ladder.

Write the difference in the next box.

This is your new number.

Find the difference between your new number and the next number on the ladder.

Continue to the bottom.

Which start number finishes on 5972?

You can use the space below for your working.

[ ]

Hint: The numbers are near multiples of 1000.

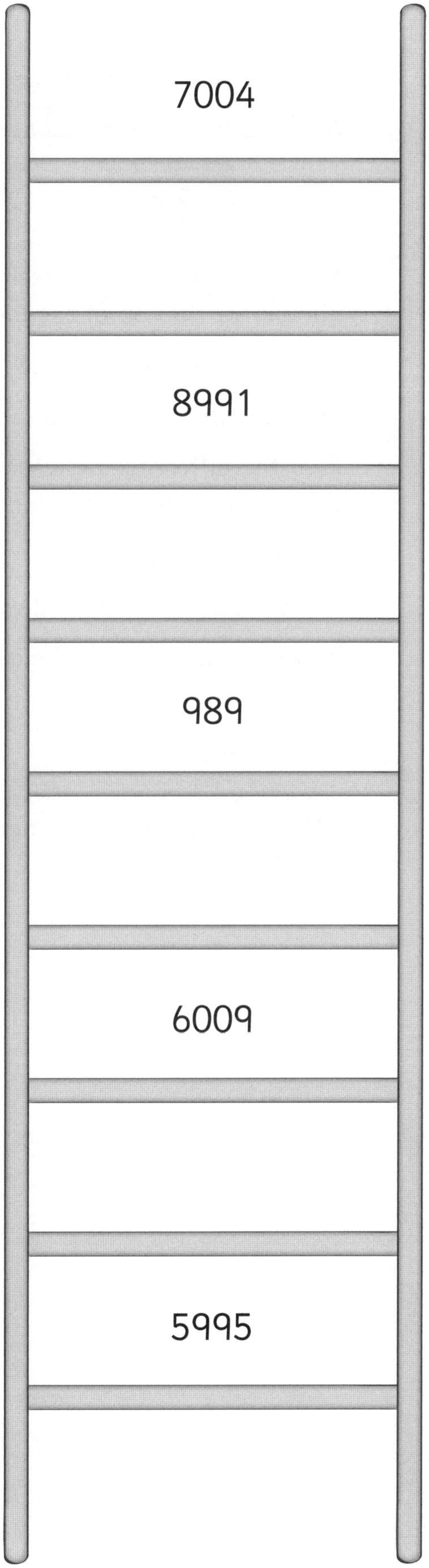

3 Choose a number.

3.8 **5.1** **4.9** **4.2** **6.0**

Find the difference between your number and the number at the top of the ladder.

Write the difference in the next box.

This is your new number.

Find the difference between your new number and the next number on the ladder.

Continue to the bottom.

Which start number finishes on 4.2?

You can use the space below for your working.

[ ]

Hint: The numbers are near multiples of 1.

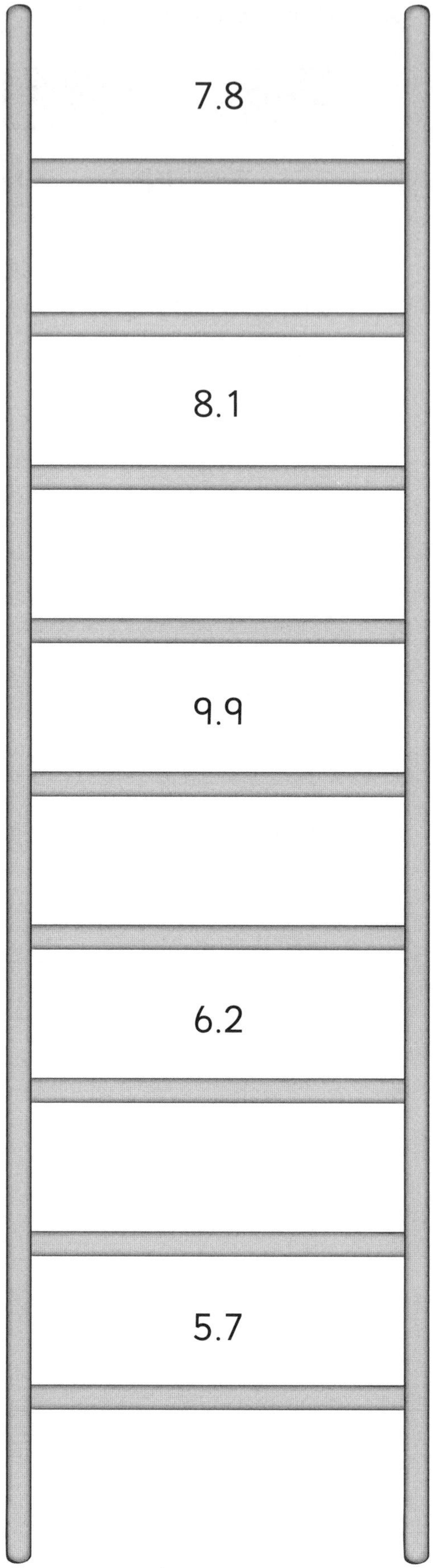

Fractions, decimals and percentages

Remember

To solve these problems you need to understand that a percentage is the number of parts out of 100.

You can use fractions, decimals and percentages to describe the same quantity. Some useful equivalences are:

$\frac{1}{2} = 0.5 = 50\%$, $\frac{1}{10} = 0.1 = 10\%$.

These equivalences can be used to work out other equivalences.

You will need: red, blue, green and yellow pencils or pens

Vocabulary

per cent, percentage, equivalent fraction, mixed number, improper fraction

1 Shade 40% of the squares red.

Shade $\frac{3}{10}$ of the squares blue.

Shade 0.1 of the squares green.

Shade the rest yellow.

Describe the yellow part of the grid as a fraction, a decimal and a percentage.

fraction: ☐ decimal: ☐ percentage: ☐

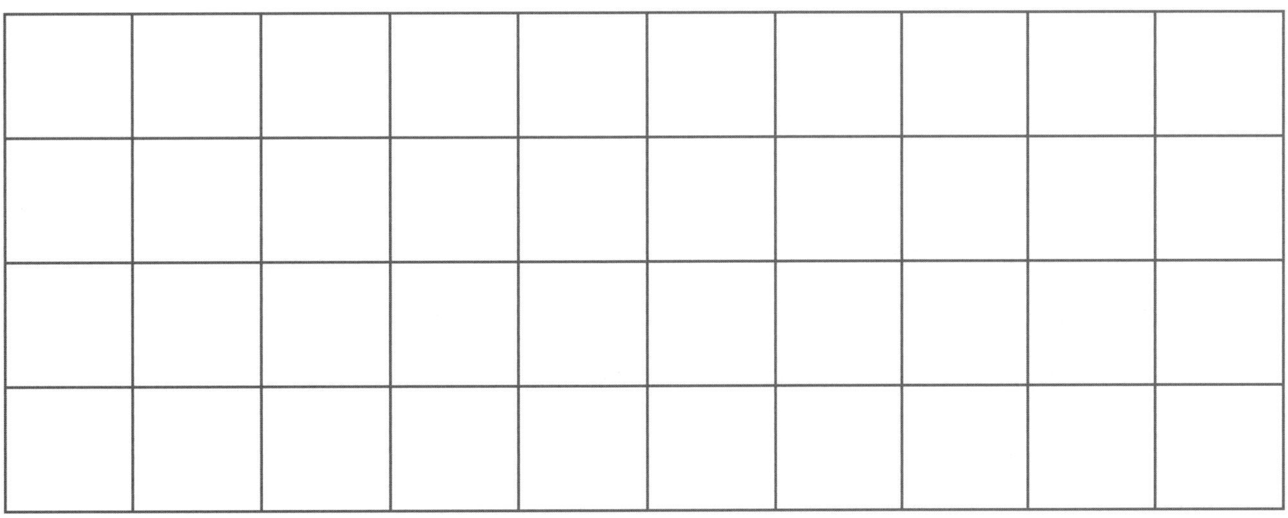

Hint: First check how many squares there are in the grid.

2 Divide 90 by each of these numbers.

1, 2, 3, 4, 5, 6, 7, 8, 9, 10

Circle the divisor that leaves $\frac{1}{4}$ as a remainder.

Divide 66 by each of these numbers.

1, 2, 3, 4, 5, 6, 7, 8, 9, 10

Circle the divisor that leaves $\frac{1}{2}$ as a remainder.

Divide 72 by each of these numbers.

1, 2, 3, 4, 5, 6, 7, 8, 9, 10

Circle the divisor that leaves $\frac{1}{5}$ as a remainder.

Divide 57 by each of these numbers.

1, 2, 3, 4, 5, 6, 7, 8, 9, 10

Circle the divisor that leaves $\frac{1}{3}$ as a remainder.

Hint: Check whether the fraction remainder is equivalent to the fraction you are looking for.

3 Mark these numbers on the number line as accurately as you can.

0.5 | $\frac{2}{5}$ | $\frac{3}{4}$ | $\frac{11}{4}$ | $\frac{9}{8}$ | $2\frac{1}{2}$ | $\frac{8}{10}$ | 2.4 | 0.9 | 1.25 | $1\frac{9}{10}$ | $\frac{13}{5}$

Hint: Try converting the improper fractions to mixed numbers.
Try converting the fractions to decimals to compare and order them.

4 Zina is selling necklaces.

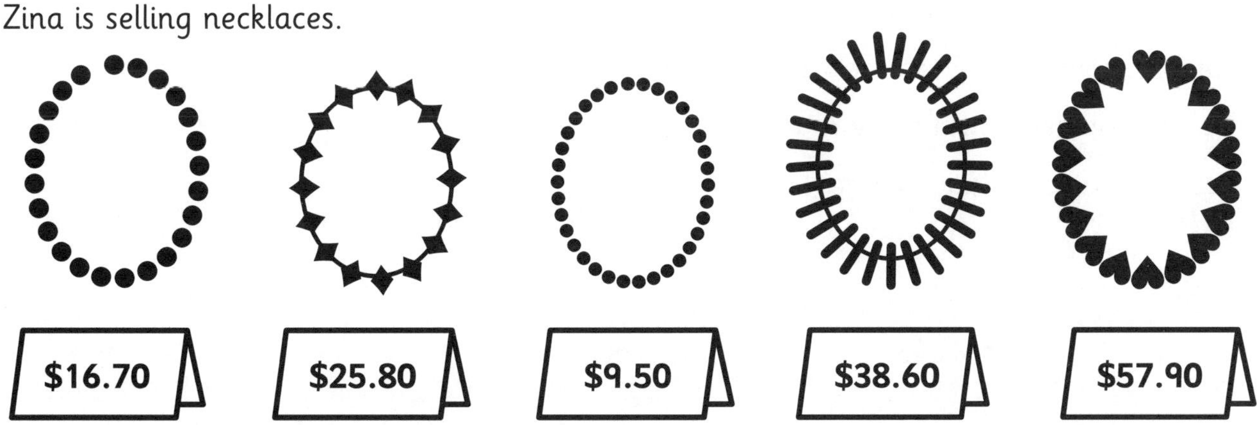

She keeps 20% of the price of each necklace.

If she sells all of the necklaces, how much money will she keep? ☐

Lulu, who makes the jewellery, keeps $\frac{1}{4}$ of the price.

Who keeps more of the money, Zina or Lulu? ☐

Hint: To find 20%, first find 10% then double it.

Calculations and brackets

Remember
The parts of a calculation that are enclosed in brackets are calculated first.

Vocabulary
brackets, order of operations, consecutive

1 Add these six consecutive numbers.

657, 658, 659, 660, 661, 662

2 **Consecutive numbers – a game for two players.**

Each player chooses a three-digit number.

They write down the number and the next five consecutive numbers.

Players find the total of their numbers.

Then they spin the spinner to find a target number.

The player with the total closest to the target number on the spinner wins the round.

Choose new numbers to play the next round.

Spin the spinner to find a new target number.

The first player to win three rounds is the winner.

Record your calculations here.

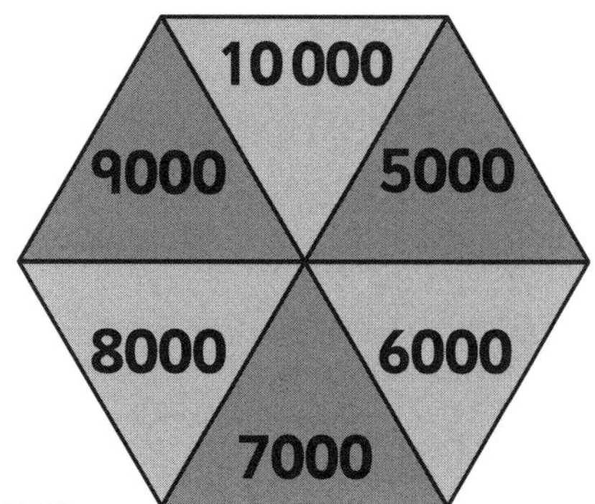

Hint: Use a written method to add the numbers.
Find out who is closest to the target number by subtracting each number from the target to find the difference.

3 Put brackets into the calculations to make the number sentences true.

$2 \times 3 + 5 = 16$

$8 + 20 \div 4 = 7$

$9 \times 7 - 2 = 45$

$26 - 56 \div 8 = 19$

$7.4 \times 2 + 9 = 23.8$

$19.6 \div 5.3 - 3.3 = 9.8$

$81 - 8.6 \div 2 + 73.3 = 150$

$6 \times 4 + 6 \times 4 = 48$

4 Write number sentences with brackets, using any numbers or operations, to make these target numbers.

= 44.82

= 12.05

= 35.71

= 97.63

Hint: Try to use each operation (+, –, ×, ÷) in at least one of the questions.

Ratio and proportion

Remember

Use **proportion** to describe the size of one part compared to the whole, for example,

'In every packet of 12 sweets three are orange', or '$\frac{1}{4}$ of the sweets are orange'.

Use **ratio** to describe the size of one part compared to another part, for example, 'For every nine red sweets there are three orange sweets,' or 'for every three red sweets there is one orange sweet.'

You will need: coloured pens or pencils

Vocabulary

ratio, proportion

1 How much milkshake syrup should Ali add to each glass so that they all have the correct ratio and all taste the same?

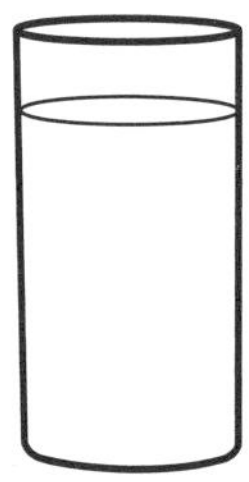

700 ml
Syrup needed:

245 ml
Syrup needed:

350 ml
Syrup needed:

875 ml
Syrup needed:

Milkshake recipe:
Mix 1 part syrup to 7 parts milk

What is the proportion of syrup in the whole milkshake as a fraction?

Hint: You could use a four-cell table, e.g.

Amount of milk (ml)	Amount of syrup (ml)
7	1
700	?

2 Toy building bricks come in a small pack with:

20 red bricks

10 yellow bricks

5 black bricks

4 white bricks

1 blue brick.

Describe the proportion of each colour as a fraction of the pack.

red:

yellow:

black:

white:

blue:

Draw a larger set of bricks in the same proportions.

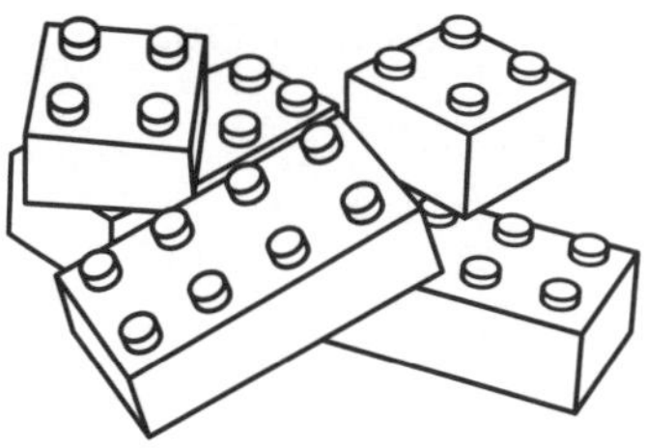

Hint: Proportion is used to compare a part to the whole.
First work out how many bricks there are in total.

Angles and triangles

Remember

Angles are measured in **degrees**. The symbol for degrees is °. Angles less than 180° can be classified as **acute**, **obtuse** or **right angles**.

When measuring angles, line up the protractor correctly and use the correct scale.

If an angle measures between two 5° intervals, round to the closer mark to measure to the nearest 5°.

Angles on a straight line total 180°.

You will need:
a protractor,
equilateral triangles from resource 2, pages 77–78

Vocabulary

acute angle, obtuse angle, right angle, straight angle, equilateral triangle, scalene triangle, isosceles triangle

1 For each of these angles:

- circle whether it is obtuse, acute or a right angle
- estimate the size of the angle
- measure the angle, to the nearest 5°.

obtuse/acute/right angle

Estimate __________

Measurement __________

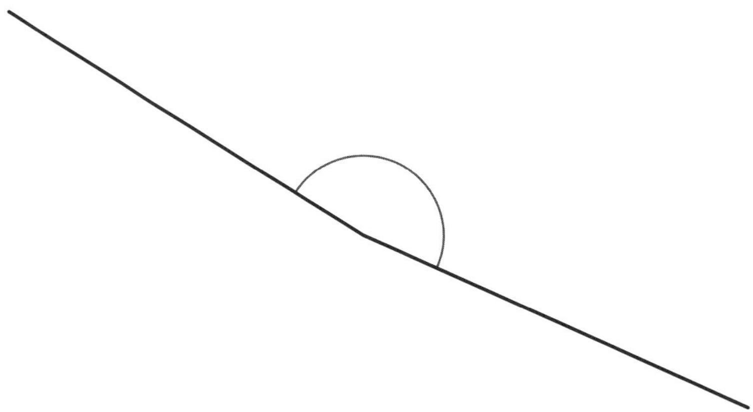

obtuse/acute/right angle

Estimate __________

Measurement __________

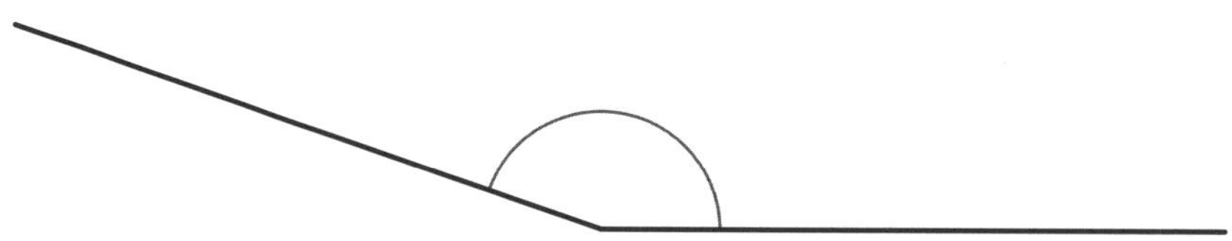

obtuse/acute/right angle

Estimate __________

Measurement __________

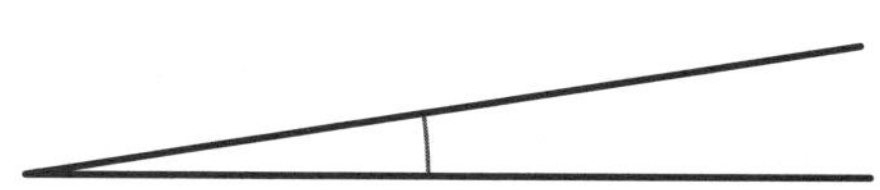

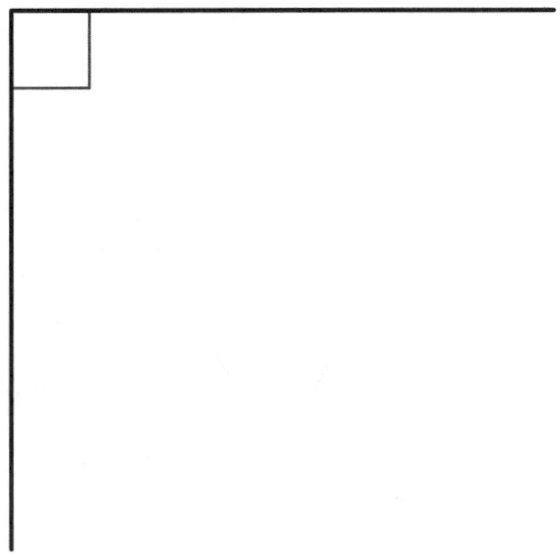

obtuse/acute/right angle
Estimate _________
Measurement _________

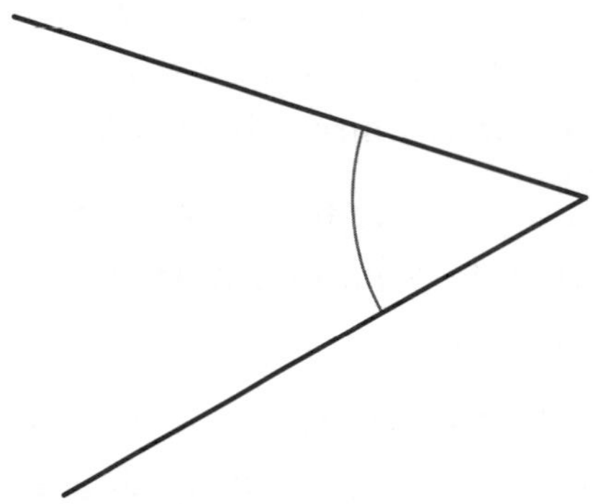

obtuse/acute/right angle
Estimate _________
Measurement _________

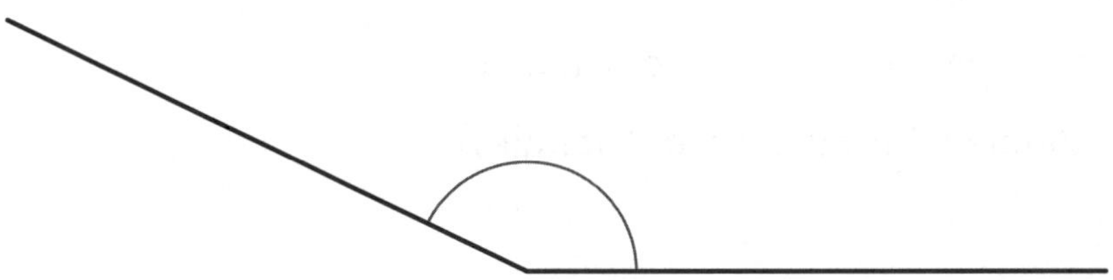

obtuse/acute/right angle
Estimate _________
Measurement _________

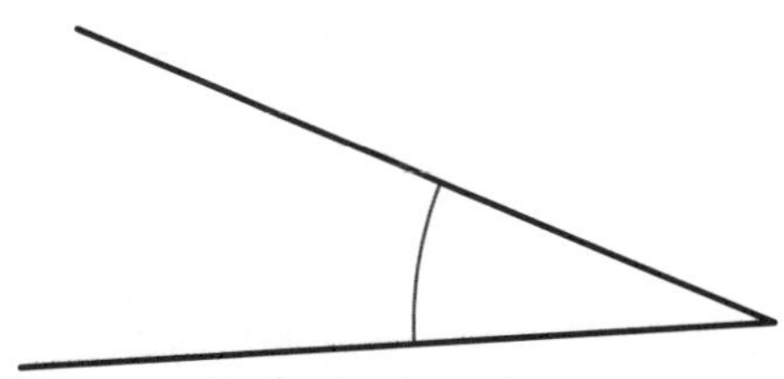

obtuse/acute/right angle
Estimate _________
Measurement _________

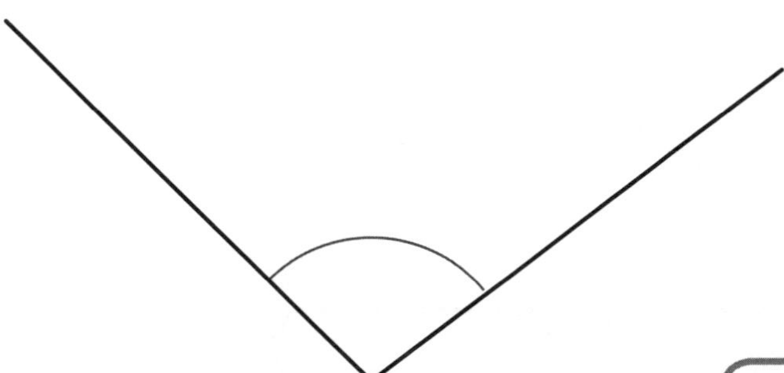

obtuse/acute/right angle
Estimate _________
Measurement _________

Hint: Some of these angles are not exactly multiples of 5°. Record their measurements to the nearest 5°.

2 Cut out equilateral triangles of different sizes, from the resource sheet. Put the triangles together in different ways to make larger equilateral triangles.

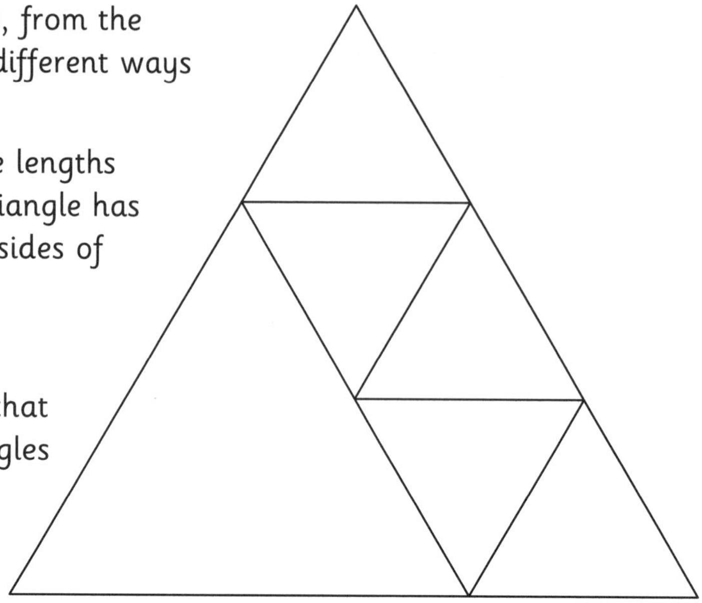

For example, this equilateral triangle has side lengths of 9 cm. It is made from six triangles. One triangle has sides of length 6 cm and the other five have sides of length 3 cm.

Choose an investigation.

- What different side lengths will triangles that you make with the set of equilateral triangles on the resource sheet have?
- Is it possible to make an equilateral triangle from any number of smaller equilateral triangles?
- Put some triangles of the same size together to make larger triangles. What size of larger triangles can you make? How many smaller triangles do you need to make each larger triangle?
- Can you make a larger isosceles triangle with equilateral triangles?
- Can you make a larger scalene triangle with equilateral triangles?

Describe what you have found out.

Hint: Work systematically.
Stick the triangles you make on the page, or sketch or photograph them.
Choose a way to record what you find. A table is useful for recording.

3 Andre is cutting planks of wood to make a platform.

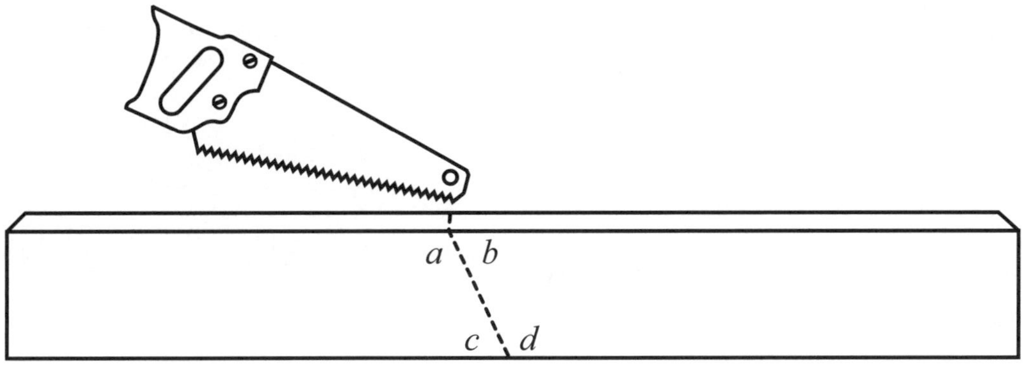

Measure the angle labelled a.

a = ☐

Calculate the size of the angle labelled b without measuring.

b = ☐

Measure the angle labelled c.

c = ☐

Calculate the size of the angle labelled d.

d = ☐

What do you notice?

Draw another cut at a different angle on the plank.

Measure and calculate the angles made by the cut.

What do you notice?

Symmetry

Remember

Lines of reflective symmetry are mirror lines.

Rotate a shape about its centre to find rotational symmetry.

You will need: protractor, mirror, colouring pens or pencils

Vocabulary

rotational symmetry,
order of rotational symmetry

1 Explore the number of lines of reflective symmetry, and where to find the lines of reflective symmetry on regular polygons.

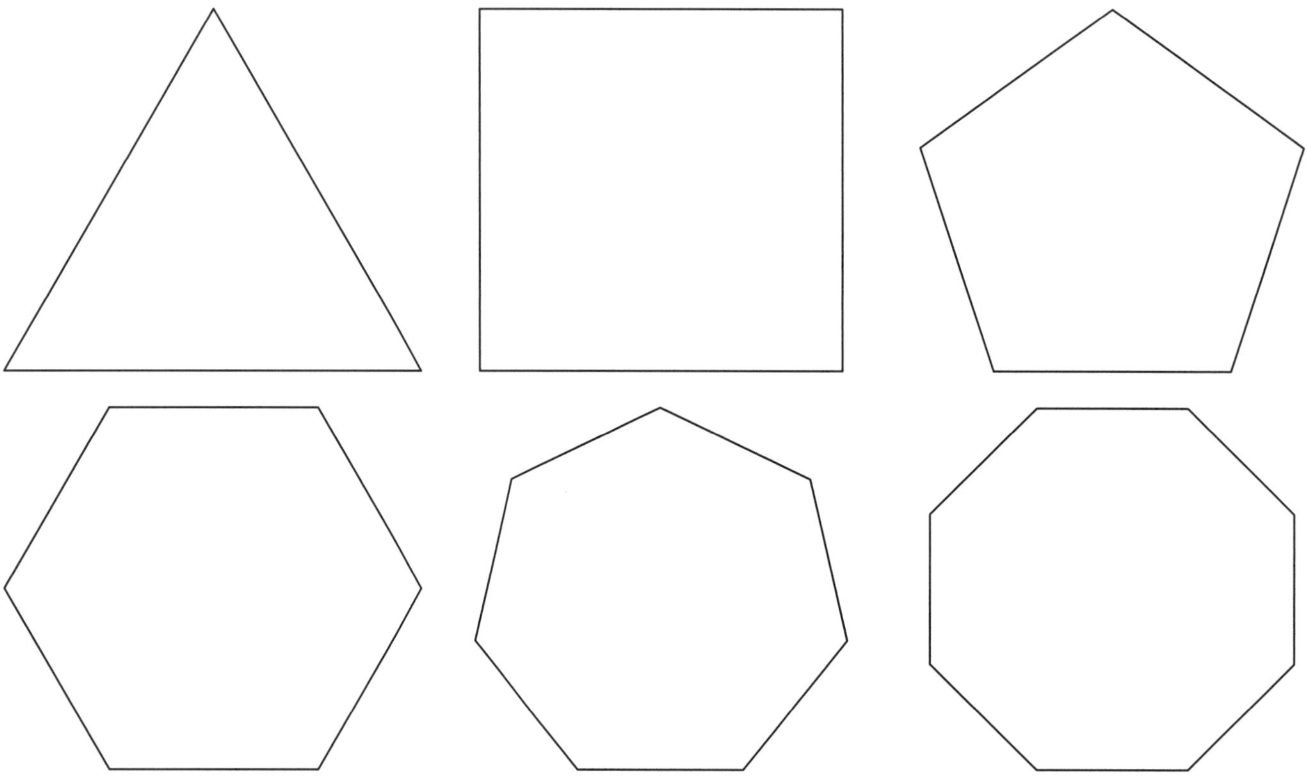

Investigate the difference in position of lines of symmetry on regular polygons with even and odd numbers of sides.

Write your findings here.

Hint: Mark which of the shapes have even, and which have odd, numbers of sides.

2 These are regular polygons. They have rotational symmetry.

When the shape is rotated about its centre it matches the original every time a corner matches the place a corner was before.

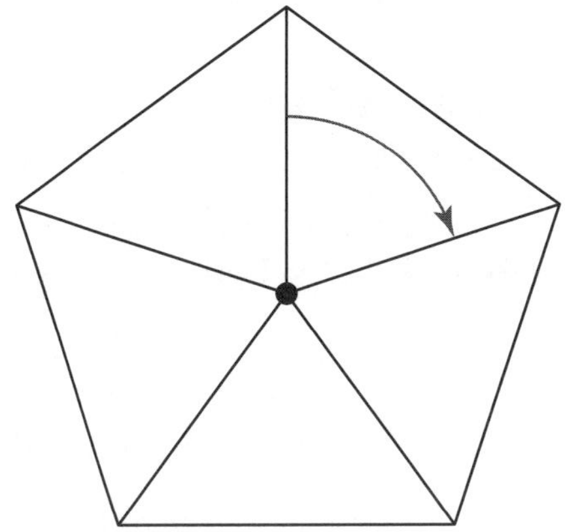

Estimate what angle the pentagon has to rotate to match its original position. [ ]

Use a protractor to measure the angle the pentagon has to rotate to match its original position. [ ]

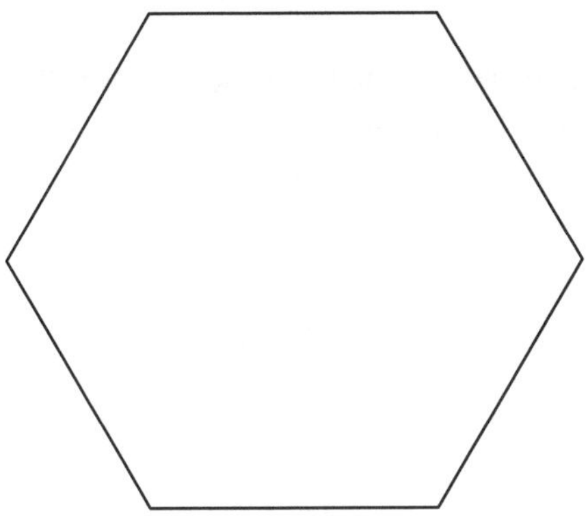

Estimate [ ]

Measure [ ]

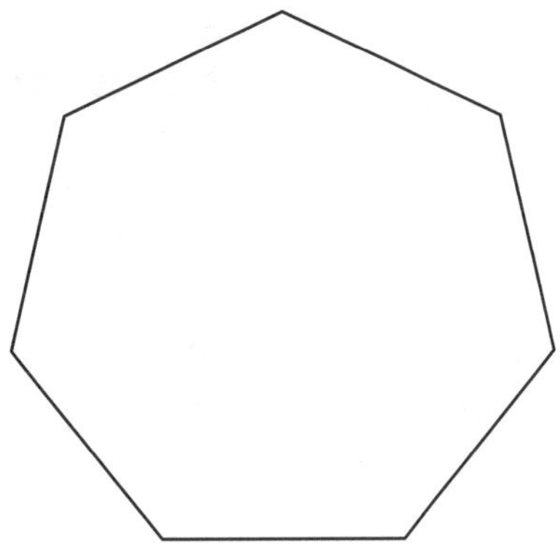

Estimate [ ]

Measure [ ]

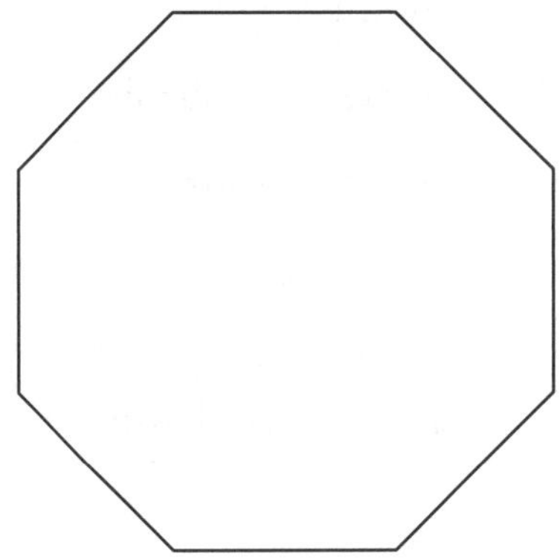

Estimate [ ]

Measure [ ]

3 Choose four colours. Use coloured pencils or pens to shade in the squares and half squares marked with a star (*).

Reflect the pattern over the mirror lines and colour all the squares to make a pattern with two lines of symmetry.

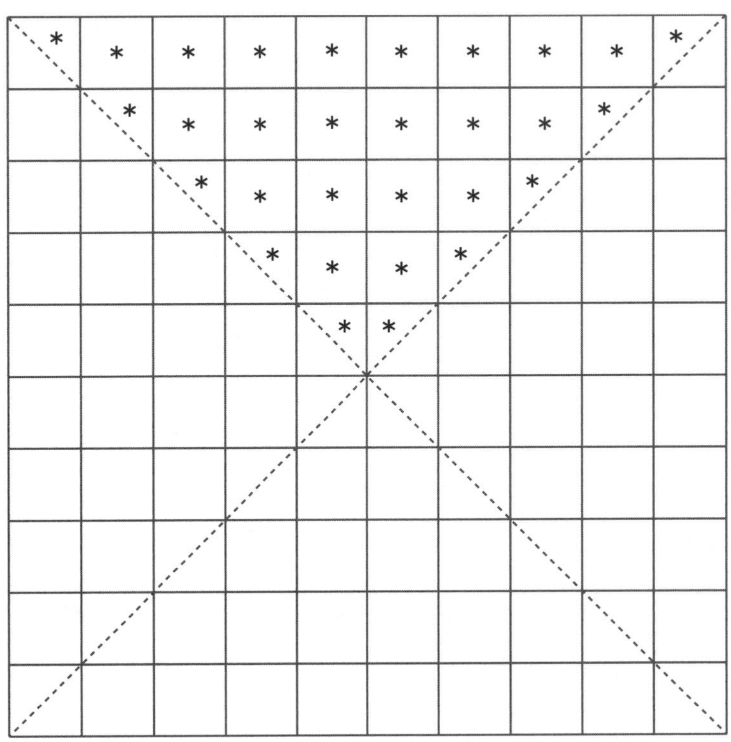

Hint: Use a mirror to check the reflection.

3D shapes and nets

Remember

A **net** is a 3D shape unfolded flat.
Visualise how a net will make a 3D shape by imagining folding the net along the lines.

You will need: resources 3 and 4, pages 79–82, coloured pencils in blue, green, yellow, purple, red and orange, ruler, thin card, scissors, sticky tape

Vocabulary
prism, pyramid

1 Copy resource 3 onto thin card.

Colour the first net so that faces that are these colours do not share an edge:

blue and green

yellow and purple

red and orange

Do the same with each net.

Hint: Faces are the flat squares that make up the cube.
Edges are the lines where the faces touch.
If faces do not share an edge then those colours are not next to each other on the cube.

Cut out and fold the nets to check that the faces have been coloured according to the rules above. Unfold the nets and stick them here.

2 This is the net of an open cube.

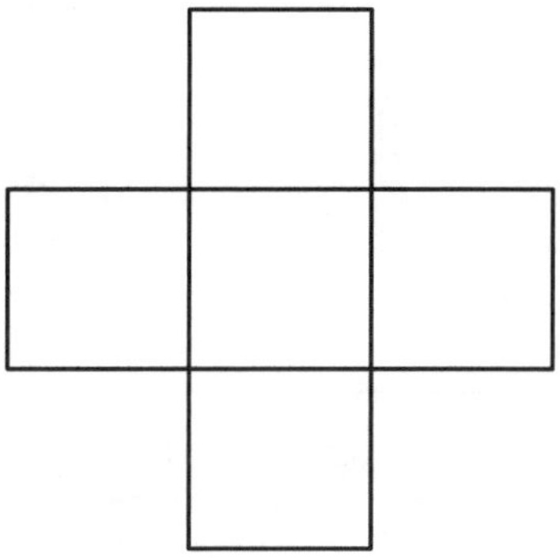

Open cube

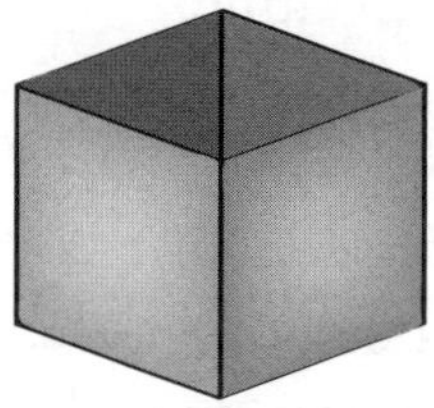

Sketch nets for an open pentagonal prism, an open hexagonal prism, an open heptagonal prism and an open octagonal prism.

Use regular polygon templates, a ruler, thin card, scissors and sticky tape to construct your open prisms.

Hint: Each net of an open prism has one fewer face than the whole prism. Use the open prisms you have made as pots to store things in.

Position and movement

Remember
The first coordinate tells you the horizontal position and the second tells you the vertical position of the point on the grid.

You will need: a ruler

Vocabulary
oblique, transformation

1 Follow the instructions below to translate the lettered squares on the grid.

Shade the squares to which they are translated.

Hint: +2 horizontally means move 2 to the right and –2 horizontally means move 2 to the left. +2 vertically means move 2 up and –2 vertically means move 2 down.

				D						M	T
N		B	C			P				Q	
A											H
E											
F											
											J
											R
	S	L				O		K			
					I		G				

A +2 horizontally
B –4 vertically
C –6 vertically
D –7 vertically
E +7 horizontally
F +5 horizontally
G +7 vertically
H –2 horizontally
I +6 vertically
J –4 horizontally

K +4 vertically
L +3 vertically
M –2 horizontally, then –3 vertically
N +2 horizontally, then –3 vertically
O +1 horizontally, then +4 vertically
P +3 horizontally, then –3 vertically
Q –3 horizontally, then –5 vertically
R –6 horizontally, then +2 vertically
S +4 horizontally, then +6 vertically
T –2 horizontally, then –5 vertically

What word is revealed in the shaded squares? ______

2 Plot (0, 1) and (6, 4) on the grid.

Use a ruler to draw a line from (0, 1) to (6, 4).

The line passes through two more points on the grid where the gridlines cross.

What are those points?

[ ] [ ]

Draw a rectangle on the grid with two sides parallel to the line from (0, 1) to (6, 4).

Reflect your rectangle over the line.

Hint: Use a ruler to check that two sides of the rectangle are parallel to the line.

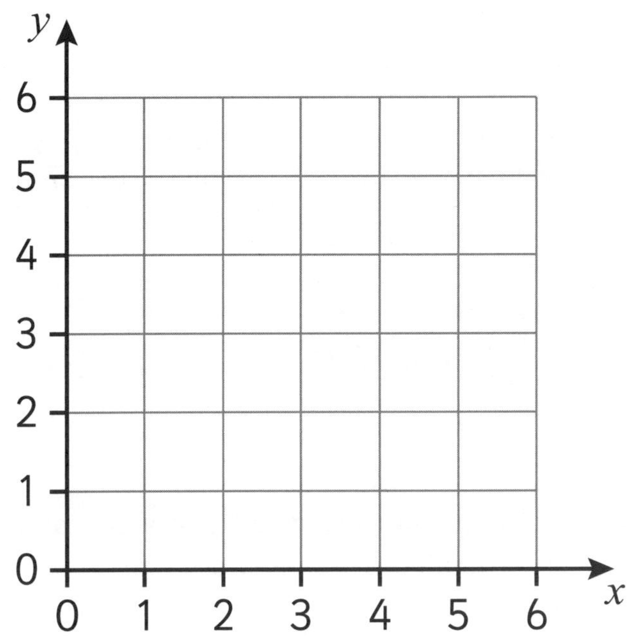

3 Translate triangles A, B, C and D onto triangle X.

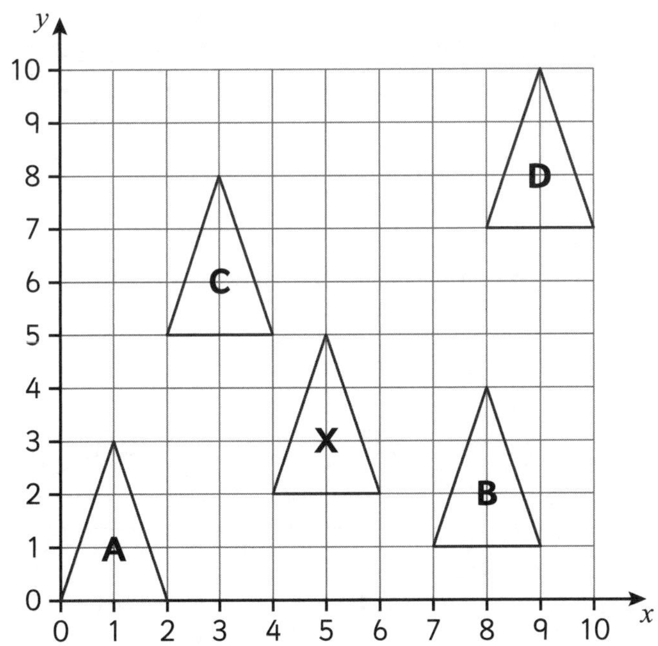

A: [ ] horizontal, [ ] vertical

B: [ ] horizontal, [ ] vertical

C: [ ] horizontal, [ ] vertical

D: [ ] horizontal, [ ] vertical

Hint: Choose one point on the triangle and work out how many spaces horizontally and how many spaces vertically that point needs to move to be translated onto the same point on triangle X.

Capacity

Remember

To solve these problems you need to be able to read a scale accurately. Work out what each unlabelled division mark on the scale stands for and remember to use the correct units for capacity.

1 litre = 1000 ml
0.1 litre = 100 ml
0.01 litre = 10 ml
0.001 litres = 1 ml

You will need:
ruler

Vocabulary
capacity,
liquid volume, litre,
millilitre

1 Draw lines from the water containers to the circle that shows each measurement rounded to the nearest litre.

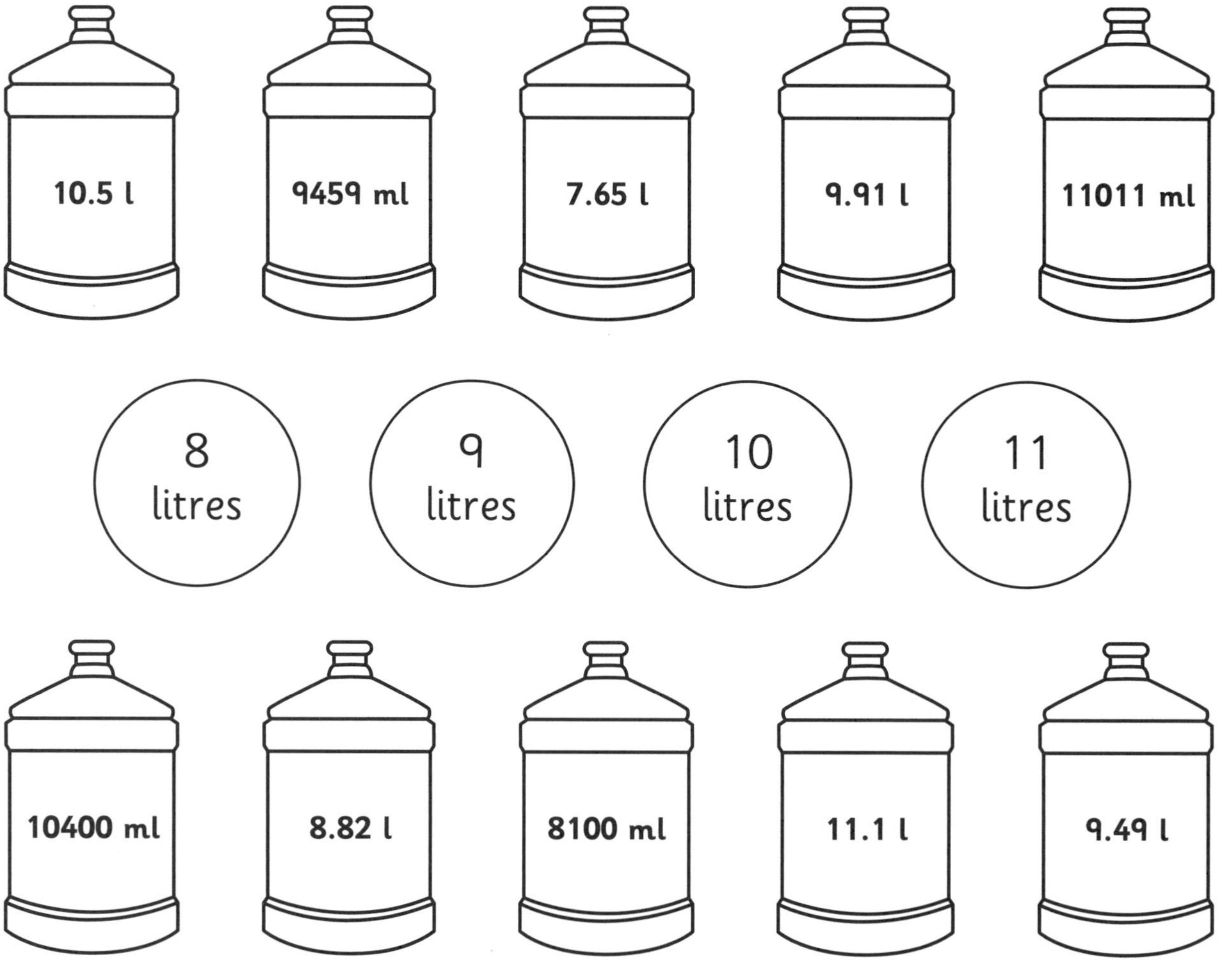

Hint: Sketch or imagine a number line. Consider where the measurement would appear on the line and which would be the nearest whole-litre interval.

2 Estimate the amount of liquid in each container.

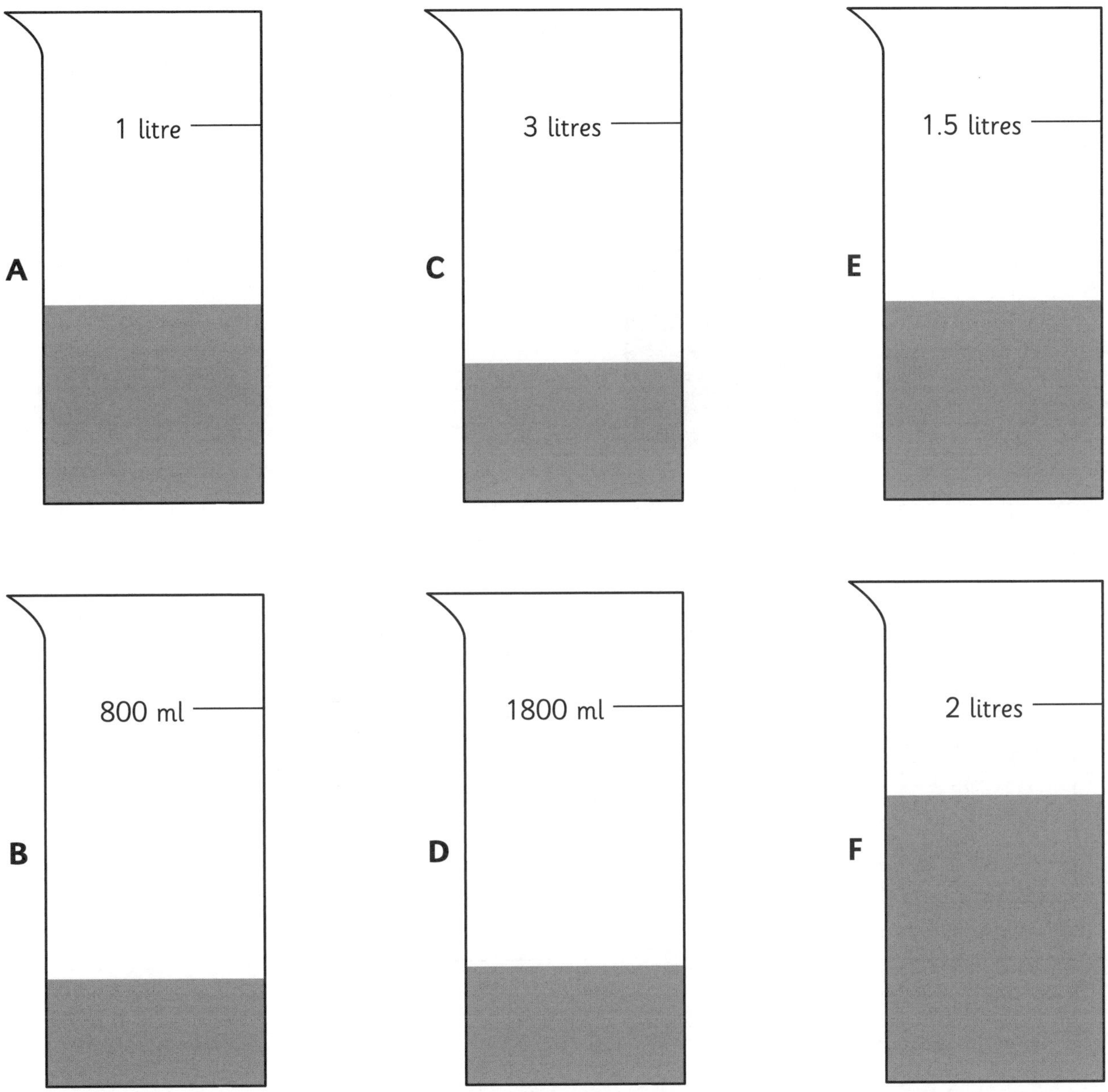

A: ______ C: ______ E: ______

B: ______ D: ______ F: ______

Order the amounts of liquid from the least to the greatest.

______, ______, ______, ______, ______, ______

Hint: Estimate what fraction of the container is full.
Work out that fraction in millilitres or litres.

3 Draw the same amount of liquid in each of these measuring cylinders.

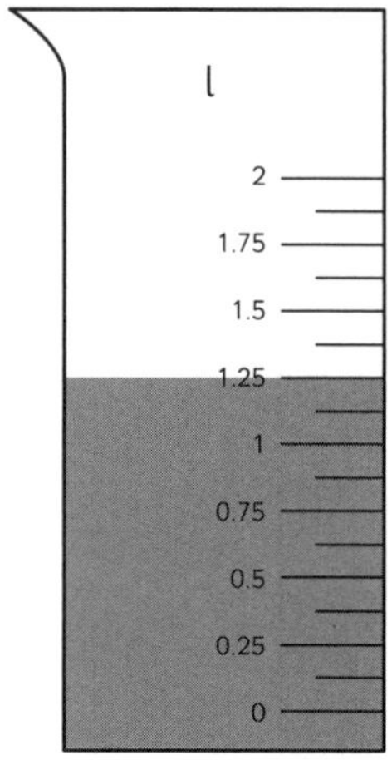

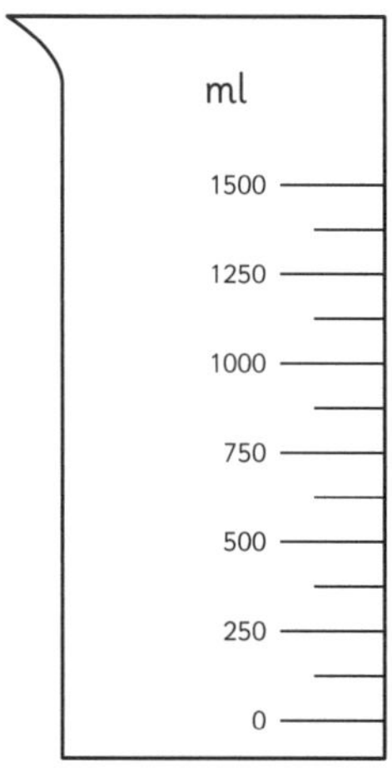

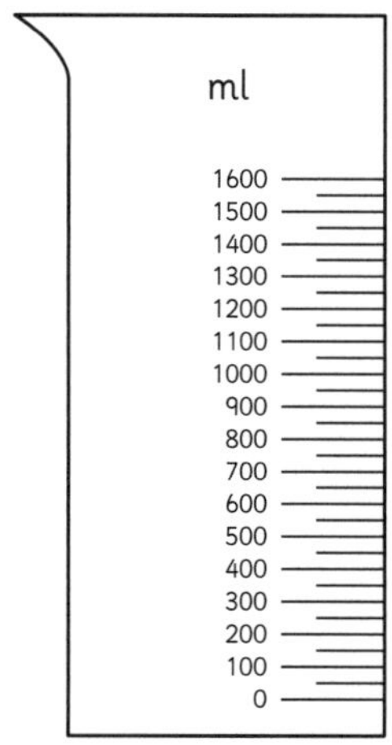

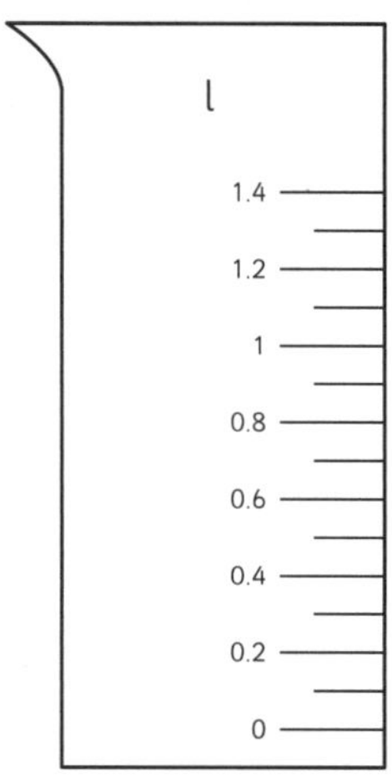

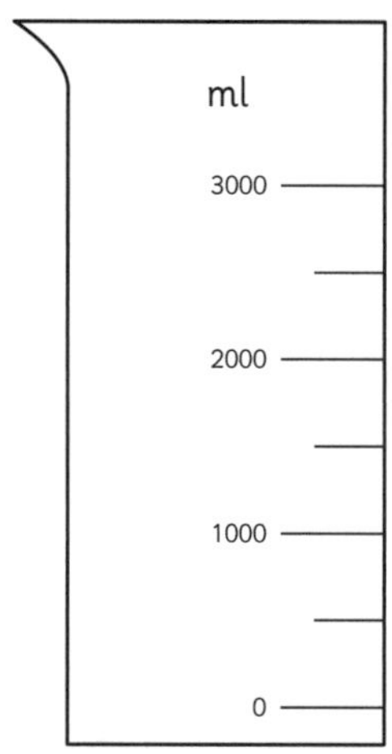

Hint: Work out the amount of liquid in both litres and millilitres. Draw the level of liquid in each container with a ruler.

Area and perimeter

Remember

The area of a rectangle can be worked out by multiplying its length by its width.

Area is measured in square units, e.g. square centimetres (cm^2).

You will need:
ruler, protractor

Vocabulary

area, perimeter, square centimetre (cm^2)

1 This dodecagon (12-sided polygon) is made from squares that each has a perimeter of 28 cm.

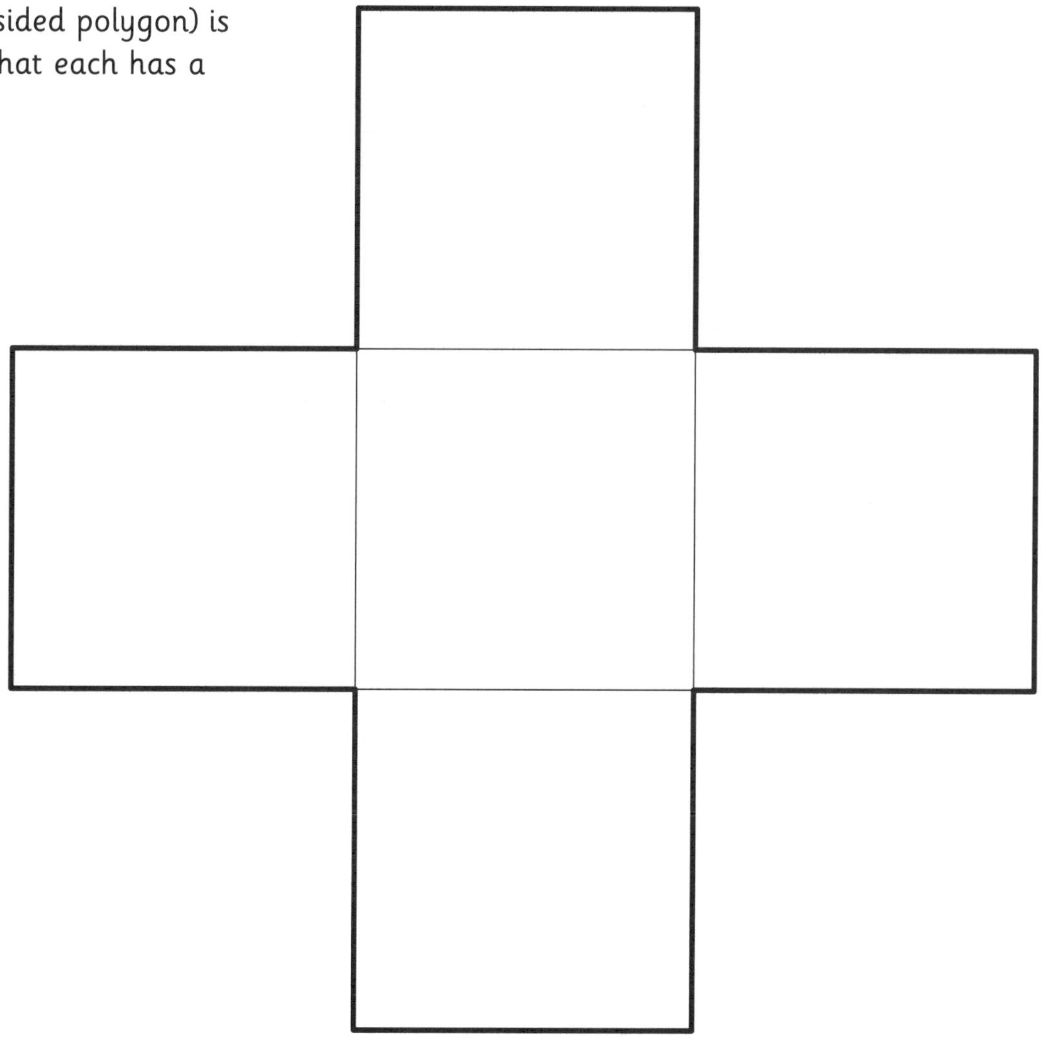

What is the area of the dodecagon? ☐

What is the perimeter of the dodecagon? ☐

Hint: Work out the length of one side of a square first.

2 This rectangle is made from smaller rectangles that measure 9 cm long by 3 cm wide.

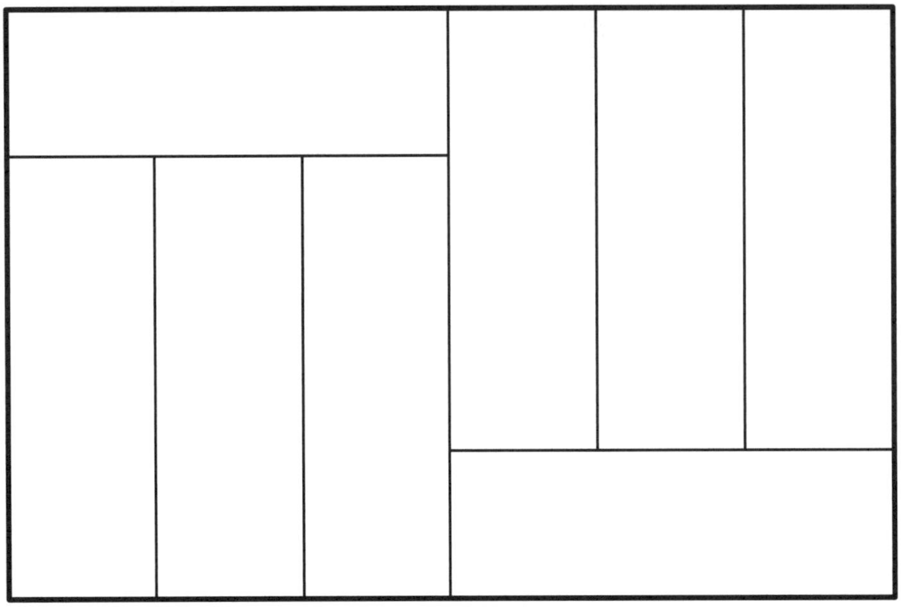

What is the area of the larger rectangle? [ ]

What is the perimeter of the larger rectangle? [ ]

Hint: Start by working out the area of one small rectangle.

3 Investigate the possible length and width of a rectangle that has an area of 48 cm^2 and a perimeter of 38 cm.

Draw a rectangle with this area and perimeter accurately. Label your drawing.

Hint: Find different lengths and widths that multiply together to make the area. Use a protractor to make sure that the corners of your rectangle are 90°.

Problems and puzzles

Remember

Use ordered lists and tables to help you solve problems systematically.

To solve problems using logic use sentences such as:
'If this is true, then this must also be true,' or
'If this is true, then this must not be true.'

Vocabulary

logic, systematically

1 Read what Mia is saying.

$$3 \times 6 = 18$$

The product of the digits in 36 is 18. 18 is half of 36.

Find two different numbers that match each description.

(a) A two-digit number in which the product of the digits is one-third of the two-digit number.

Use this space to record the numbers you try.

(b) A two-digit number in which the sum of the digits is one-third of the product of the digits.

Use this space to record the numbers you try.

Hint: Think how you will find two-digit numbers with a digit sum or product that can be divided by three without a remainder. Try to work systematically.

2 2 and 3 are **consecutive** numbers.

2 squared equals 4.

3 squared equals 9.

The difference between 2 squared and 3 squared is 5.

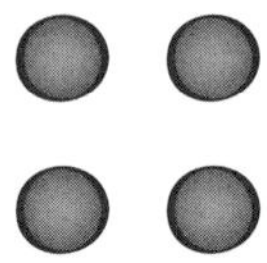

2 squared equals 4

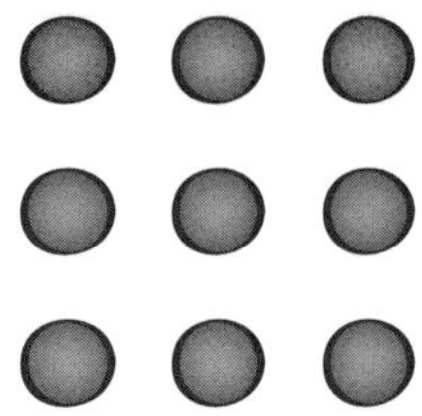

3 squared equals 9

Investigate the differences between different pairs of consecutive squared numbers.

What do you notice?

3 Which three **consecutive** numbers give the product closest to 1000 when multiplied together?

Use this space to record the consecutive numbers that you try.

How do you know that you have found the product closest to 1000?

4 Each shape in the grid represents a number.

Work out the numbers represented by the shapes to find the missing totals.

■	●	■	●	= 34
●	▲	■	▲	= ☐
▲	■	■	▲	= ☐
●	▲	■	●	= ☐
= ☐	= ☐	= 36	= 30	

Hint: You could start by working out the number that is represented by ■.

5 Milly, Lily, Sara and Tara need to meet next week, but they cannot find a day when they are all able to get together.

Sara cannot meet on Wednesday, Thursday or Saturday.

Tara can only meet on Tuesday, Wednesday or Saturday.

Milly cannot meet on Monday, Tuesday or Saturday.

Lily is only available on Monday, Thursday and Saturday.

No one is able to meet on Friday.

Find each pair a day when they can meet.

	Monday	Tuesday	Wednesday	Thursday	Friday	Saturday	Sunday
Milly							
Lily							
Sara							
Tara							

Hint: Use the table to help you organise the information.

6 Each year Vijay plants trees in his orchard.

In the first year he planted 1 tree, in the second year he planted 2 trees, in the third year he planted 3 trees, in the fourth year he planted 4 trees.

He continued using the same pattern for many more years.

Fourth year

In which year did he first have over 500 trees in his orchard?

Hint: Work out and record the total number of trees that are in the orchard each year.

Resource 1
Place-value charts

100 000	200 000	300 000	400 000	500 000	600 000	700 000	800 000	900 000
10 000	20 000	30 000	40 000	50 000	60 000	70 000	80 000	90 000
1000	2000	3000	4000	5000	6000	7000	8000	9000
100	200	300	400	500	600	700	800	900
10	20	30	40	50	60	70	80	90
1	2	3	4	5	6	7	8	9

100 000	200 000	300 000	400 000	500 000	600 000	700 000	800 000	900 000
10 000	20 000	30 000	40 000	50 000	60 000	70 000	80 000	90 000
1000	2000	3000	4000	5000	6000	7000	8000	9000
100	200	300	400	500	600	700	800	900
10	20	30	40	50	60	70	80	90
1	2	3	4	5	6	7	8	9

Resource 2
Triangles

Resource 2 Triangles (continued)

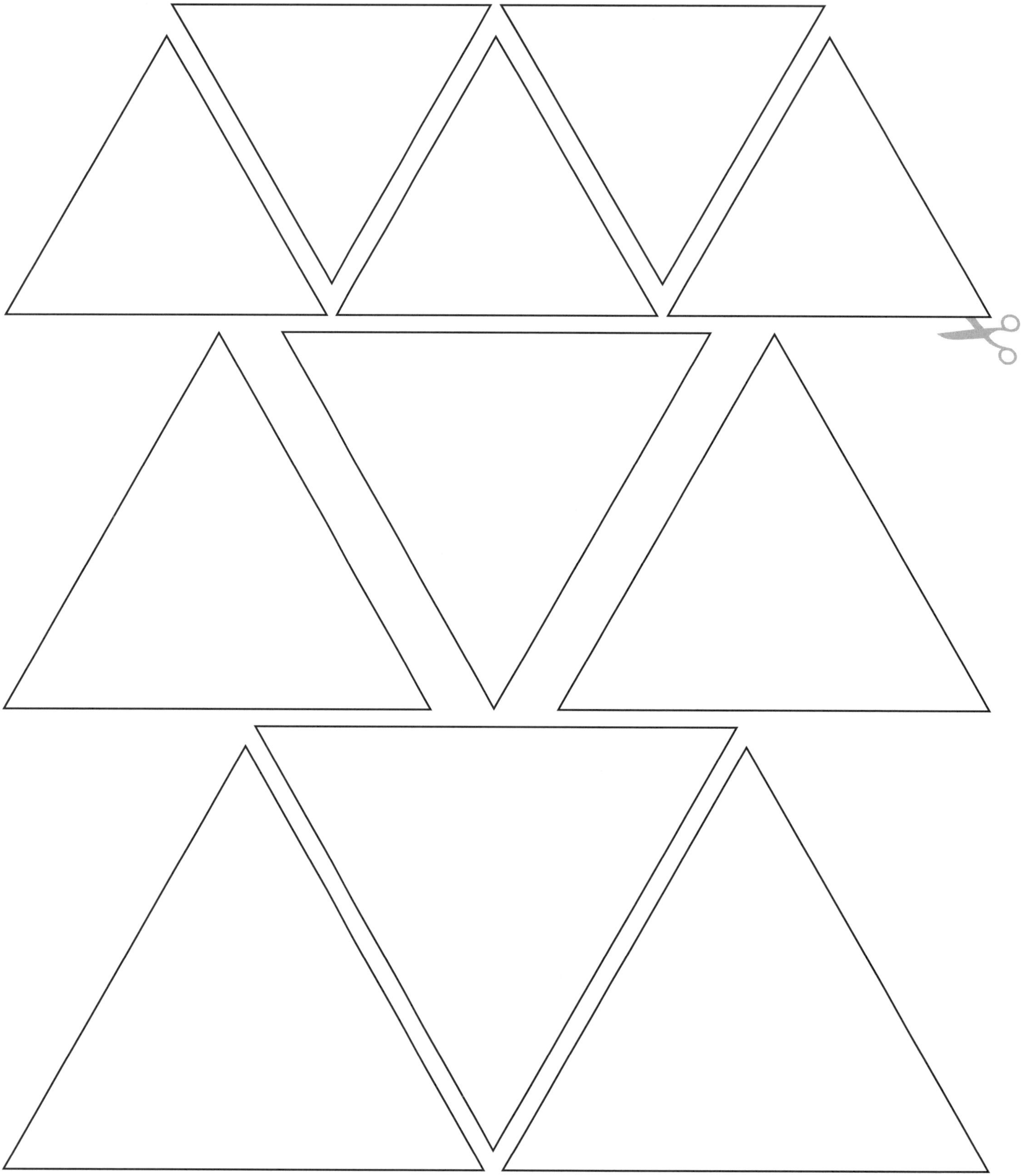

Resource 3
Nets of cubes

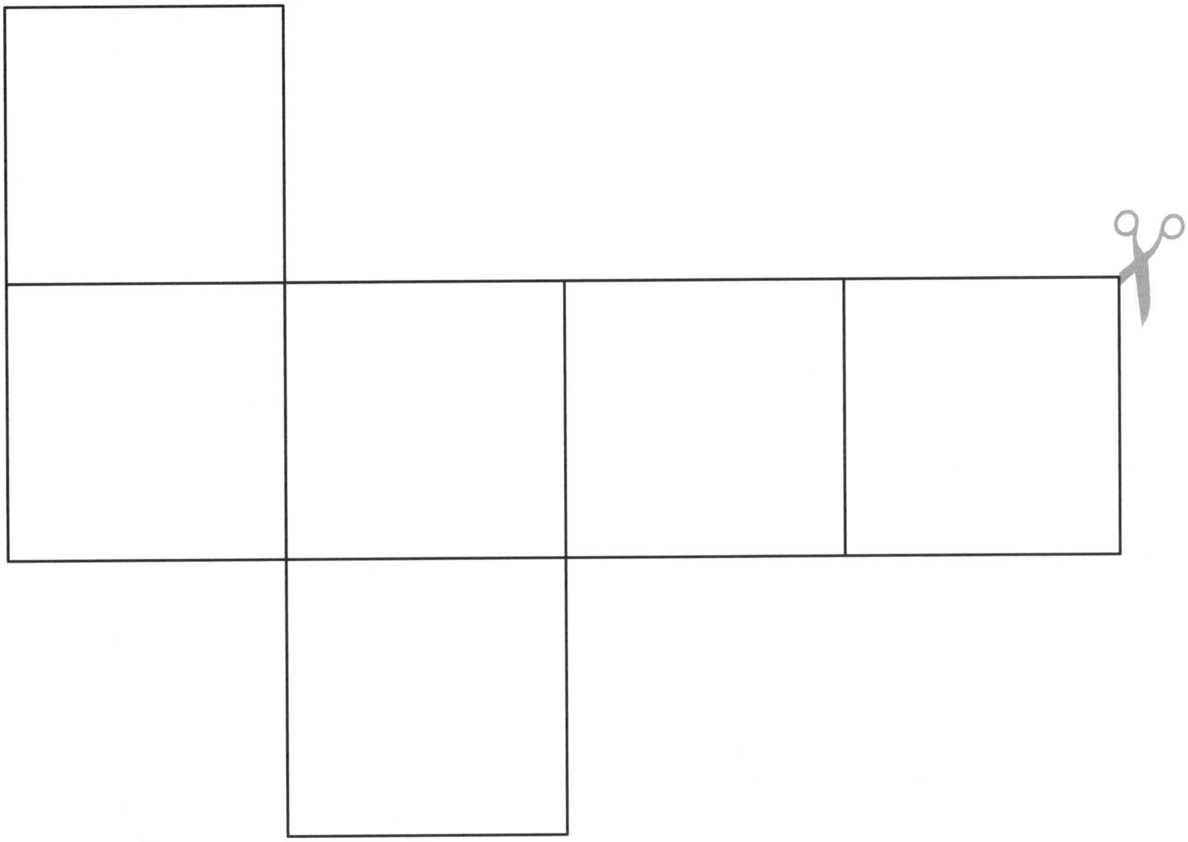

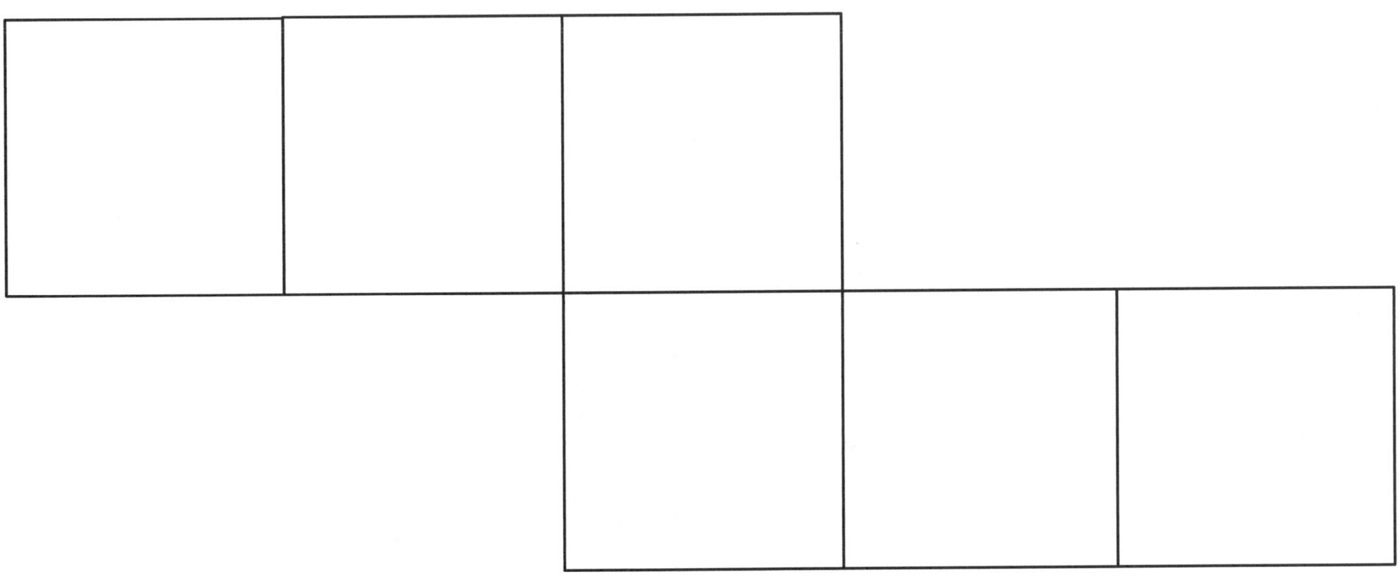

Resource 3
Nets of cubes (continued)

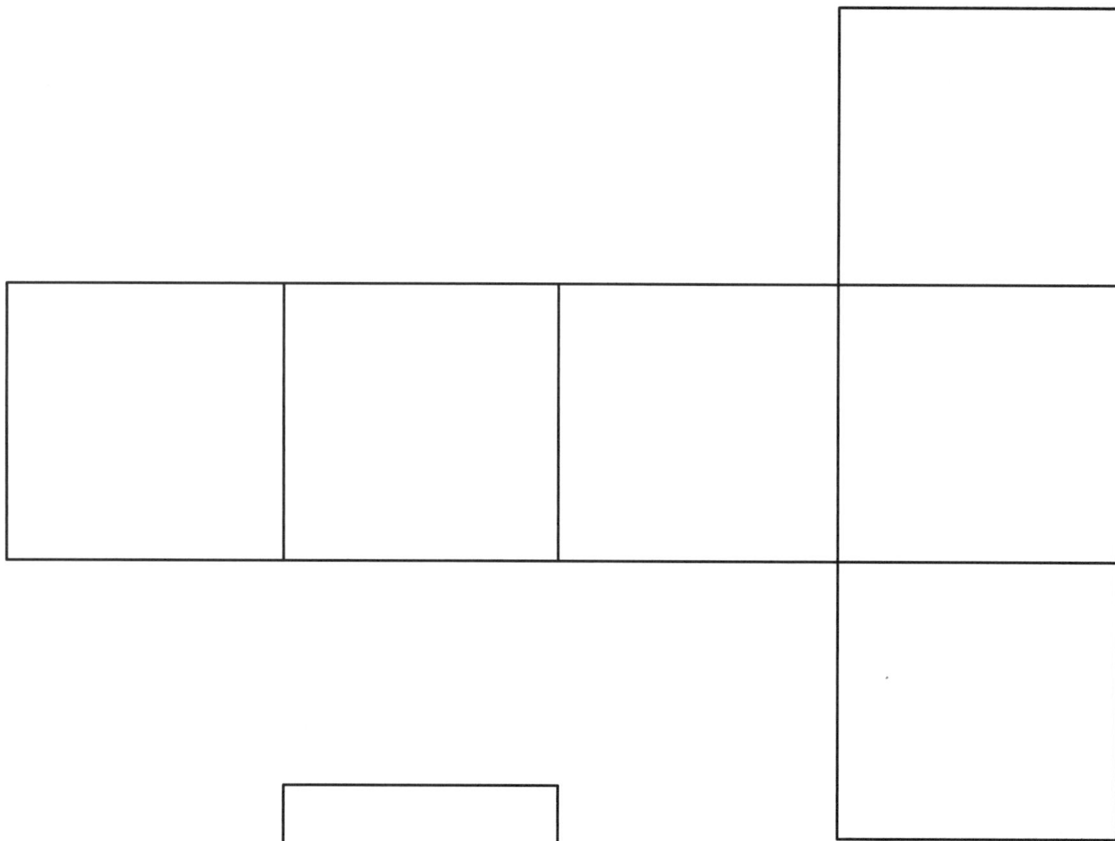

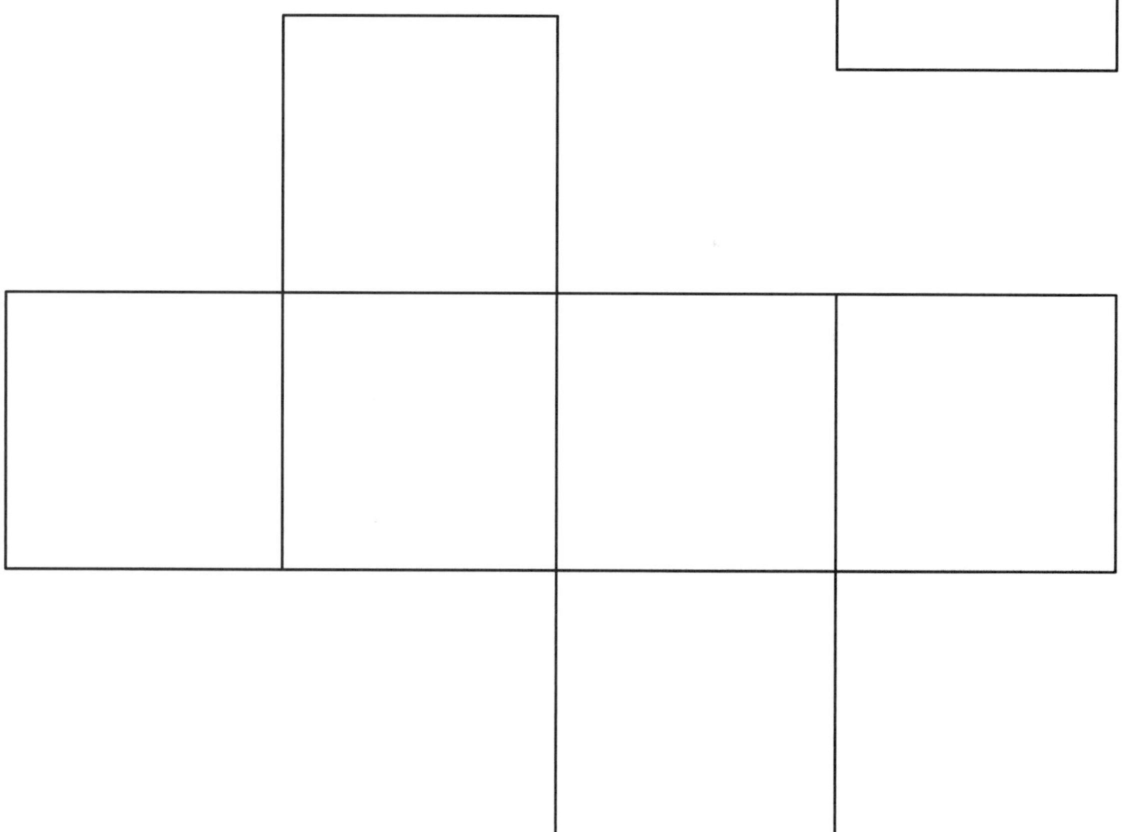

Resource 3
Nets of cubes (continued)

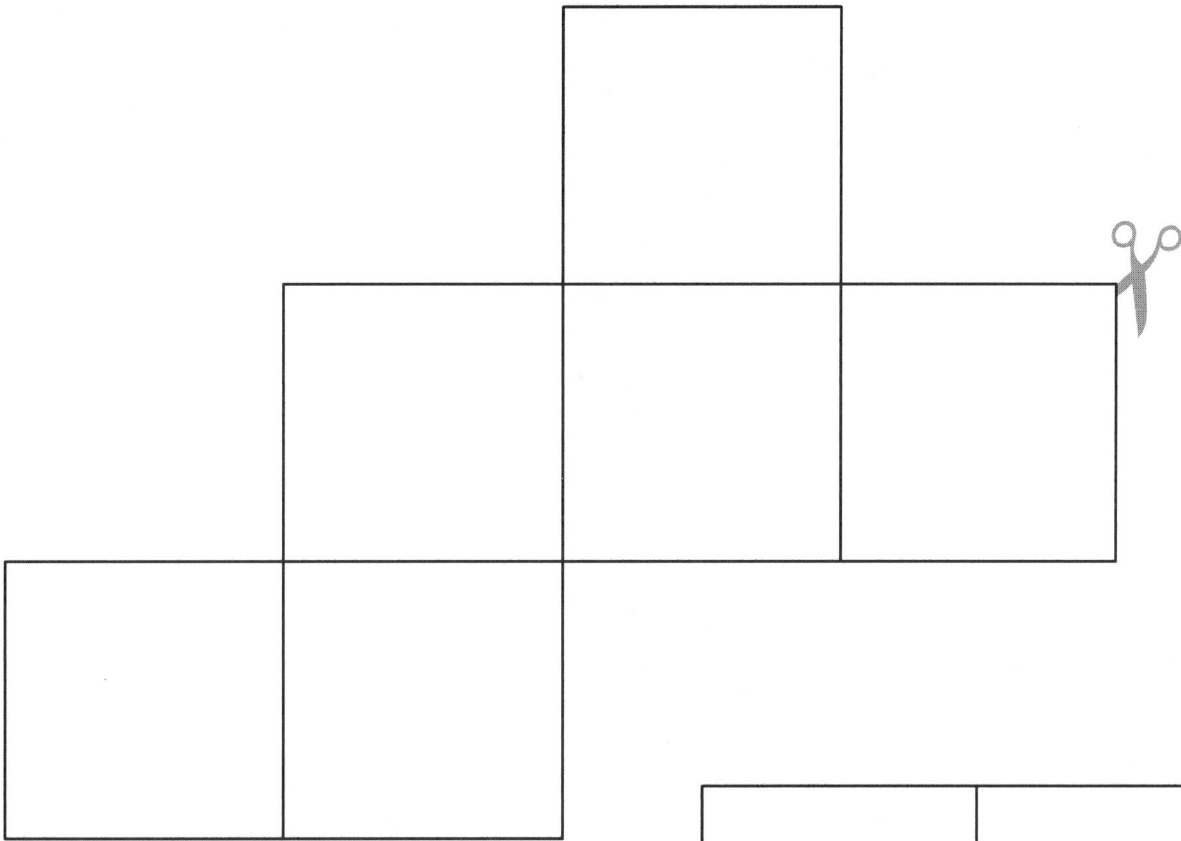

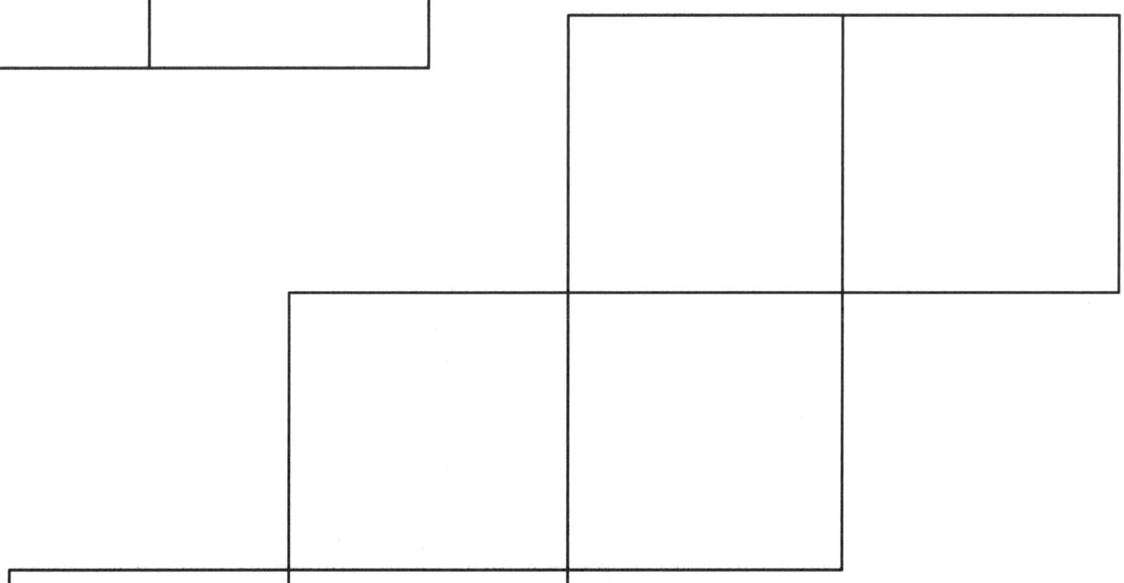

Resource 4
Polygons

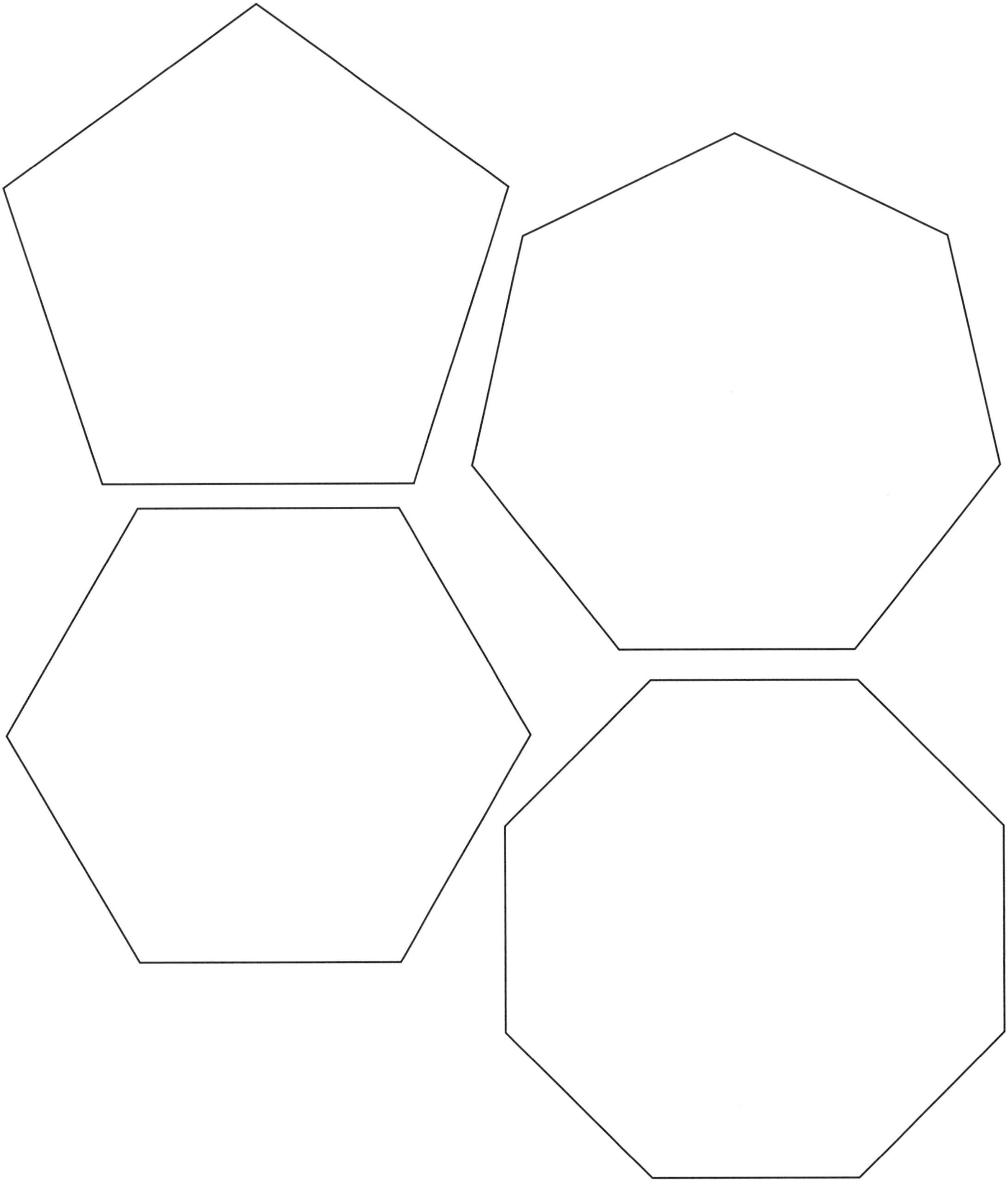

Answers

Page 4 Place value and ordering

1 Game

2 854 940

3 74 922, 88 043, 609 999, 658 107, 742 229, 841 624

700 000, 50 000, 9000, 600, 20, 3 circled in the place-value chart

759 623

4 Game

Page 7 Rounding

1 Check that the numbers match the section labels in the Venn diagram.

2 5000 m, 5396 m, 5000 m

The largest and smallest possible perimeters both round to 5000 m, so all the other possible perimeters must also round to 5000 m

3 Rob: $13 000; Ravi:$13 800; Ravi received more.

Page 9 Addition and subtraction

1 Largest total is 360. There is more than one way to make 360, e.g. 90 + 81 + 72 + 63 + 54

Smallest total is 180. There is more than one way to make 180, e.g. 10 + 29 + 38 + 47 + 56

2 423 g + 89 g + 237 g + 251 g

3 624, 103.4, 58.7, 87.6

4 The lengths passed on the route are 21.8 m, 19.3 m, 10.1 m, 16.5 m, 22.3 m.

Page 12 Multiplication and division

1

A	63	42	24	65	41	82	63	49	70	14	35	21	7	30	12	53	B
17	36	14	10	16	23	56	28	47	53	24	65	27	70	42	21	49	35
35	70	28	52	7	21	49	41	38	7	63	35	24	14	69	45	27	52
21	62	49	24	70	57	38	14	56	21	39	56	17	29	67	21	70	14
7	41	7	36	28	65	28	49	24	47	52	21	61	28	38	49	22	28
63	17	63	30	21	59	21	68			54	14	60	14	47	70	58	7
49	41	35	56	63	32	35	63			26	49	64	70	29	56	17	63
28	3	60	51	45	39	23	55	27	39	45	70	12	63	7	28	32	49
14	70	56	15	28	42	63	7	21	70	82	42	36	56	27	45	18	70
65	34	24	70	14	16	59	56	38	40	36	28	41	14	28	21	39	56
52	38	61	49	57	43	28	14	51	14	63	7	58	45	73	35	47	21
C	14	63	56	7	21	35	23	70	21	52	35	14	63	42	70	54	D

2 54 × 72 = 3888, 68 × 39 = 2652, 83 × 46 = 3818

3 15, 23, 26, 28; 5, 1, 2, 4

4 The revealed number in the grid is 4.1.

Page 15 Multiples, square numbers and factors

1

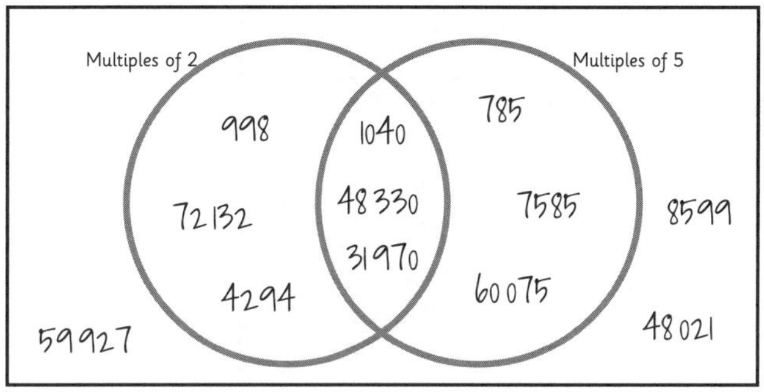

The numbers in the overlap are multiples of both 2 and 5.

2 $4 + 16 + 25 + 36 = 81$ ($2^2 + 4^2 + 5^2 + 6^2 = 9^2$)

3 72. 72 has 12 factors.

64. It is a square number, so one 'pair' of factors is the same number twice.

Page 17 Parallel, perpendicular and cuboids

1 The learner will have drawn:

A pentagon with one pair of parallel sides

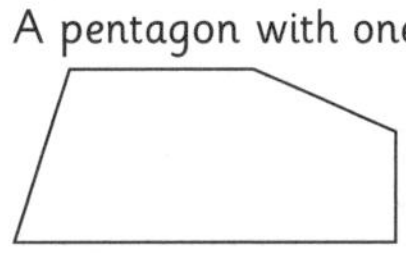

A hexagon with three pairs of parallel sides

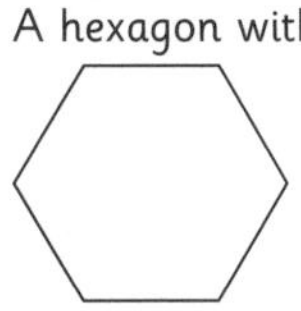

A heptagon with two pairs of parallel sides

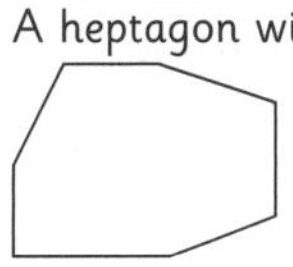

2 Length = 3 cm, Width = 2 cm, Height = 1 cm

Check that the learner can rearrange their four cuboids to match the diagrams.

Check that the learner's measurements match their cuboids.

Page 19 Mass

1 Check that the bags have the correct mass

The bags should be ordered:

20 g, 0.09 kg, 100 g, 0.25 kg, 0.4 kg, 865g, 0.9 kg, 1kg

2

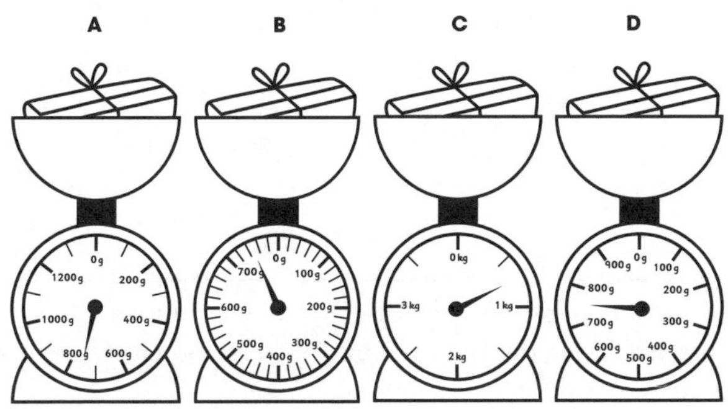

Page 21 Numbers and sequences

1 –12°C, –9°C, –2°C, 13°C, 28°C, 32°C

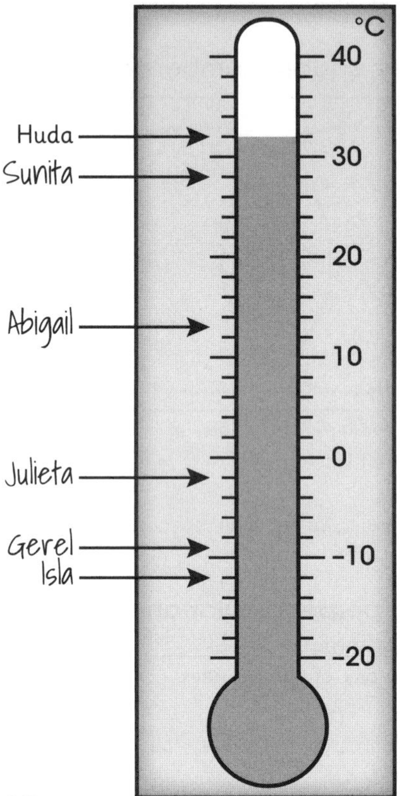

41°
10°
30°
Isla and Abigail

2 Many possible answers. One solution is:

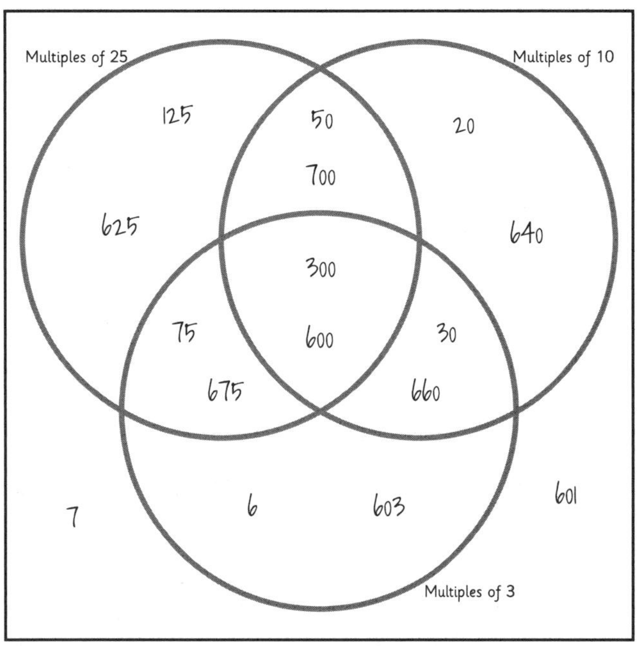

All numbers inside the 'multiples of 10' set are even.
Numbers inside the 'multiples of 3' set are odd or even, but even if they also lie in the 'multiples of 10' set.
Numbers inside the 'multiples of 25' set are odd unless they also lie in the 'multiples of 10' set.

3 68, 57, 46, 35, 24, 13, 2, –9, –20, –31
–41, –33, –25, –17, –9, –1, 7, 15, 23, 31
102, 87, 72, 57, 42, 27, 12, –3, –18, –33

4 Fahad will win.
The first spinner has only even numbers. An even number multiplied by either an even or an odd number will make an even number.

Page 24 Decimals

1 More than one solution, e.g.

0.8	0.3	0.4
0.1	0.5	0.9
0.6	0.7	0.2

2 1.59, 1.95, 5.19, 5.91, 9.15, 9.51, 51.9, 59.1, 91.5, 95.1, 15.9, 19.5
Many solutions, e.g.
1.59 < 5.19 < 9.51 < 51.9 < 95.1
91.5 > 59.1 > 9.15 > 5.91 > 1.95

3 Pairs that equal 10 are:
2.05 & 7.95, 4.3 & 5.7, 3.3 & 6.7, 8.48 & 1.52, 6.17 & 3.83, 9.3 & 0.7, 5.25 & 4.75, 6.38 & 3.62, 0.06 & 9.94, 7.59 & 2.41, 6.27 & 3.73, 7.78 & 2.22.
The extra number is 8.88. Double 8.88 equals 17.76

4

53.4	13.1	55.62	140.16
100.18	12.98	67.22	98.56
142.34	29.5	111.34	42.4
110.56	43.08	124.3	28.96
85.46	69.18	125.02	84.7

The number revealed is '3'.

5 12.98 + 125.02
124.3 + 84.7

Page 27 Addition, subtraction, multiplication and division

1 Box 1 = 35.76 + 82.04
Box 2 = 56.98 + 28.17
Box 3 = 69.53 + 23.55
Box 4 = 47.62 + 55.67
Box 5 = 74.29 + 34.81 = 109.1

2 Game

3 Numbers shaded are 100, 108, 116, 124, 132, 140, 148.
These number are all even. They are all multiples of 4. If the hundreds digit is removed they are multiples of 8.
The total is 868

4 1098 – 403 = 695

5 The statement is true. If the two-digit number is even, then squared it is even. An even number is subtracted and the result is even.
If the two-digit number is odd, then squared it is odd. An odd number is subtracted and the result is even.

Page 31 Questions, surveys, data and finding the mode

1 The questions should be useful for finding out what children would like on a picnic.

2 The bar line graph should match the information in the table. It should have a title and the axes should be labelled.

97

10 hours

Learners should write three of their own questions that can be answered using the data.

Page 34 Line graphs

1 The information in the graph should match this table:

Time	Shadow length (cm)
9 a.m.	21
10 a.m.	14.5
11 a.m.	9
12 p.m.	5.5
1 p.m.	8.5
2 p.m.	13.5

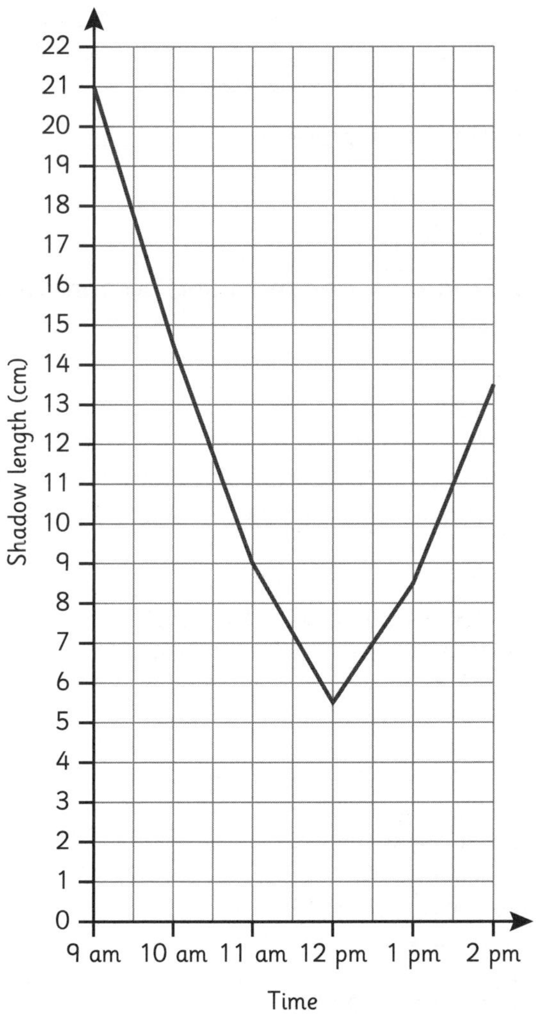

The shadow would be approximately 11 cm at half past 1.

2

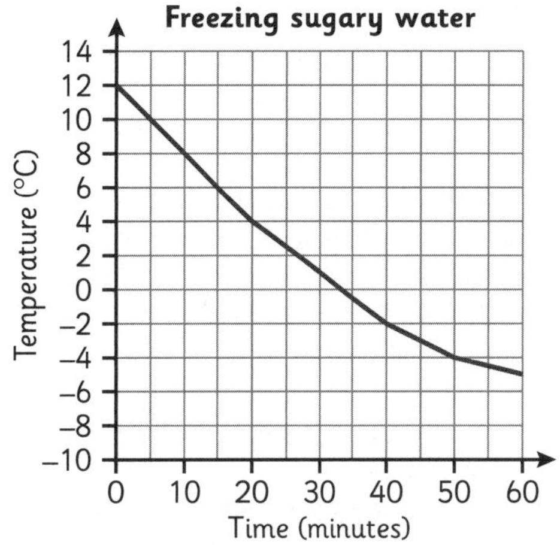

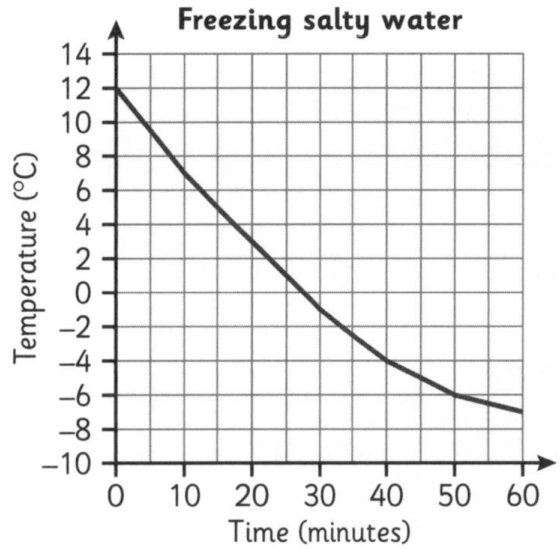

Some correct answers are:

- The salty water got colder than the sugary water.
- After 20 minutes the temperature of the salty water was one degree lower than the sugary water.
- The temperature of the salty water was below 0°C before 30 minutes, it took longer than 30 minutes for the sugary water to reach below 0°C.
- A line graph is a good choice because the intermediate points have a value that can be approximated by drawing a line between two of the points.

Page 37 Probability

1 Hexagonal spinner, 4 sections blue, 1 section green, 1 section yellow
Octagonal spinner – there is more than one solution. One possible solution is:
5 sections blue, 2 sections green, 1 section yellow.
Check that the answers 'A / B' match the coloured possible outcomes on the spinners.

2 There are many solutions. On the learner's net there must be:
- one or two negative numbers
- no multiples of 3
- three odd numbers and four or five even numbers
- three numbers greater than 5

Check the statements on the probability scale match the possible outcomes on the net.

Less than 16	Certain
Even number	Good chance
Greater than 5	Even chance
Multiple of 3	No chance

3 The probability of taking a prism from the bag is **good chance**.
The probability of taking a 3D shape from the bag is **certain**.
The probability of taking a pyramid from the bag is **poor chance**.

Page 40 Length

1 Graph should show plants measure:
Day 1 22 mm, Day 2 67 mm, Day 3 83 mm, Day 5 115 mm, Day 6 130 mm, Day 7 141 mm
Day 4 plant should be approximately 99 mm tall.

2 Holes labelled in this order (left to right): 109 cm, 1.68 m, 180 cm, 1.9 m, 2.3 m, 234 cm

3

Triangle	Coordinates	Length of shortest side to the nearest cm	Length of shortest side to the nearest mm	Length of longest side to the nearest cm	Length of longest side to the nearest mm.
A	(2, 1) (2, 3) (5, 1)	2 cm	20 mm	4 cm	36 mm
B	(8, 3) (5, 7) (8, 7)	3 cm	30 mm	5 cm	50 mm
C	(1, 5) (3, 3) (3, 8)	3 cm	28 mm	5 cm	50 mm

Page 43 Time

1 Learner's own timetable using 24-hour clock times.

2

3 228 days, Mariner 6, 11 days

4 Wednesday, if the current month has 30 days
Thursday, if the current month has 31 days
Monday, if the current month is February
Tuesday, if the current month is February and it is a leap year.

5 February; 2004, 2008, 2012, 2016, 2020, 2024, 2028, 2032, 2036, 2040, 2044, 2048, 2052, 2056, 2060, 2064, 2068, 2072, 2076, 2080, 2084, 2088, 2092, 2096

Page 46 Mental strategies

1 Game
2 4988 ends on 5972
3 4.9 ends on 4.2

Page 49 Fractions, decimals and percentages

1 fraction: $\frac{2}{10}$ or $\frac{1}{5}$
decimal: 0.2
percentage: 20%

2 8, 4, 10, 9

3 The numbers should be arranged in this order (bottom to top):
$\frac{2}{5}$, 0.5, $\frac{3}{4}$, $\frac{8}{10}$, 0.9, $\frac{9}{8}$, 1.25, $1\frac{9}{10}$, 2.4, $2\frac{1}{2}$, $1\frac{13}{5}$, $1\frac{11}{4}$

4 \$29.70, Lulu

Page 52 Calculations with brackets

1 657 + 658 + 659 + 660 + 661 + 662 = 3957

2 Game

3 2 × (3 + 5) = 16
(8 + 20) ÷ 4 = 7
9 × (7 – 2) = 45
26 – (56 ÷ 8) = 19
(7.4 × 2) + 9 = 23.8
19.6 ÷ (5.3 – 3.3) = 9.8
81 – (8.6 ÷ 2) + 73.3 = 150
(6 × 4) + (6 × 4) = 48

4 Many possible solutions, for example,
50.82 – (2 × 3) = 44.82
(26 ÷ 2) – 0.95 = 12.05
0.71 + (7 × 5) = 35.71
(100 + 95.26) ÷ 2 = 97.63

Page 54 Ratio and proportion

1 100 ml
50 ml
35 ml
125 ml
$\frac{1}{8}$

2 red: $\frac{1}{2}$
yellow: $\frac{1}{4}$
black: $\frac{1}{8}$
white: $\frac{1}{10}$
blue: $\frac{1}{40}$
Picture should represent the same proportions, but the set has been doubled, for example,
40 red bricks
20 yellow
10 black bricks
8 white bricks
2 blue bricks

Page 56 Angles and triangles

1 obtuse 170°, obtuse 160°, acute 100°, right angle 90°, acute 45°, obtuse 155°, acute 25°, obtuse 100°.

2 Learner's own investigation. They should have recorded and explained what they have found.

3 115°
65°
65°
115°
The two pairs of angles on opposite sides of the plank have the same measurements.

Page 60 Symmetry

1 In regular polygons with even numbers of sides the lines of symmetry go from corner to corner, or from the centre of a side to the centre of a side.
In regular polygons with odd numbers of sides the lines of symmetry go from corner to the centre of a side.

2 Measurement recorded should be:
pentagon: 72° (70° to the nearest 5°)
hexagon: 60°
heptagon: 51.4° (50° to the nearest 5°)
octagon: 45°

3 Learner's pattern should have two lines of symmetry, as shown by the dashed lines.

Page 62 3D shapes and nets

1 These colours are not adjacent on the cubes made by the learner:
blue and green
yellow and purple
red and orange

2 Learner will have successfully made open pentagon, hexagonal, heptagonal and octagonal prisms.

Page 64 Position and movement

1 Squares form the word 'UP'.

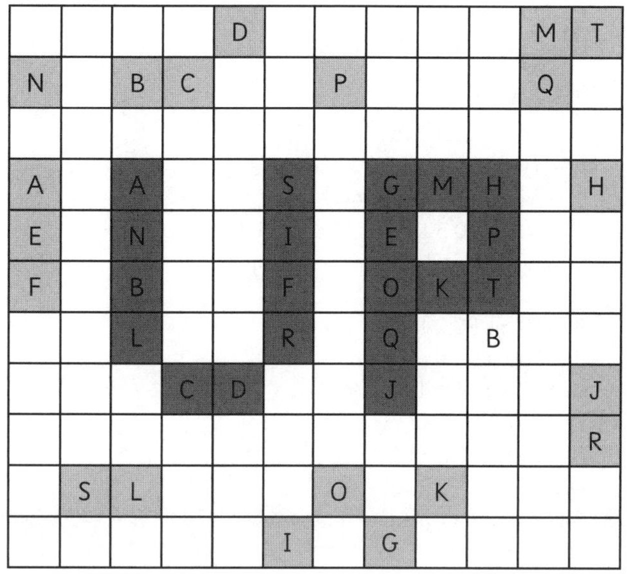

2

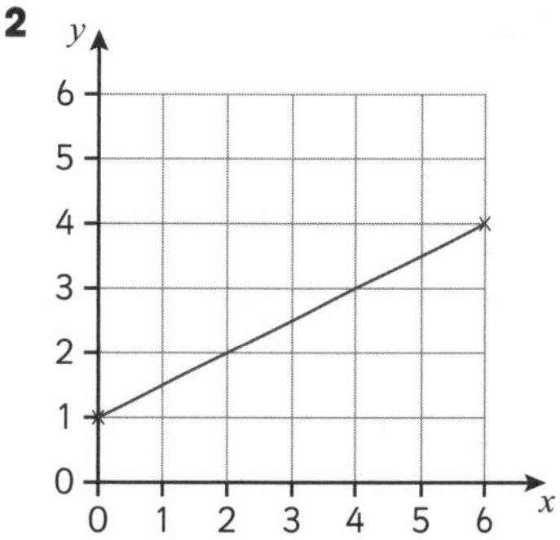

(2, 2), (4, 3)
Rectangle drawn parallel to the oblique line.
Rectangle reflected over the oblique line.

3 A: +4 horizontal, +2 vertical
B: –3 horizontal, +1 vertical
C: +2 horizontal, –3 vertical
D: –4 horizontal, –5 vertical

Page 66 Capacity

1 8 litres – 7.65 l & 8100 ml
9 litres – 9459 ml, 8.82 l & 9.49 l
10 litres – 9.91 l & 10400 ml
11 litres – 10.5 l, 11011 ml & 11.1 l

2 Estimates should be approximately:
A: 500 ml / 0.5 l
B: 200 ml / 0.2 l
C: 1000 ml / 1 l
D: 600 ml / 0.6 l
E: 750 ml / 0.75 l
F: 1500 ml / 1.5 l
Order: B, A, D, E, C, F

3 All measuring cylinders should show 1.25 litres / 1250 millilitres of liquid.

Page 69 Area and perimeter

1 Area: 245 cm^2
Perimeter: 84 cm

2 Area: 216 cm^2
Perimeter: 60 cm

3 Learner should have accurately drawn a rectangle 16 cm by 3 cm.

Page 71 Problems and puzzles

1 **(a)** 24
(b) 66

2 The difference between any pair of consecutive squared numbers is always odd.

3 9 × 10 × 11 = 990. This is closest to 1000 because the next consecutive numbers make the product 1320.

4

■	●	■	●	= 34
●	▲	■	▲	= 31
▲	■	■	▲	= 32
●	▲	■	●	= 32
= 32	= 31	= 36	= 30	

5 Milly and Lily can meet on Thursday.
Milly and Sara can meet on Sunday.
Milly and Tara can meet on Wednesday.
Lily and Sara can meet on Monday.
Lily and Tara can meet on Saturday.
Sara and Tara can meet on Tuesday.

6 In the 32nd year there will be 528 trees.